CHRISTIANITY, EVIDENCE AND TRUTH

To, Brother
Duncan,
in Christian love,

Barry Rachel.

in His Service.

Christianity Evidence and Truth

ROGER FORSTER AND PAUL MARSTON

MONARCH

Crowborough

British Library Cataloguing in Publication Data
A catalogue record for this book is available
from the British Library.

ISBN 1 85424 311 X

Produced by Bookprint Creative Services
P.O. Box 827, BN21 3YJ, England for
MONARCH PUBLICATIONS
Broadway House, The Broadway,
Crowborough, East Sussex, TN6 1HQ.
Printed in Great Britain.

*We demolish arguments and every pretension
that sets itself up against the knowledge of God,
and we take captive every thought
to make it obedient to Christ.*

(2 Corinthians 10:5)

Contents

Scene Setting
  1. About this book   11
  2. Why bother about God?   14

Evidence
  3. What is the evidence for God?   19
  4. Science: assertions and limits   23
  5. Science, origins and chance   30
  6. Has God been in touch?   44
  7. A pattern in God's dealings?   50
  8. Reliable sources?   58
  9. Dead men tell no tales   68
10. Detective work and the resurrection   75
11. I think therefore I am – I think…   81
12. It's a miracle!   90
13. The experience of God   98

Response
14. Over to you!   107

Digging Deeper: Further Reading   117

Index   121

Scene Setting

1

About this book

"So, Mr Forster, you want a consumer-desirable,
slick, high-street image for a book
taking Christianity seriously?"

What's it about?

Christianity is an active faith. It involves lifestyle commitment, experience of God, and various acts of ceremony and worship.

But it is not just some kind of 'trip' – like an alternative to cocaine or ecstasy. Christians believe that their faith is founded on truth. It is self-fulfilling, life-enhancing and (sometimes, at least!) good fun. But it also claims to be true.

Is it obvious what is meant here by 'true'? What we assume is that there is only one reality, and therefore only one truth about that reality – even though it may sometimes be described in different words. Perhaps to many this seems obvious. They just assume that there *is* a single, unique 'truth' about things – even if that truth may sometimes be difficult or impossible to know. There are, however, some others (and philosophers talk about 'post-modernism') who suggest that 'truth' is not unique but varies for different people. In an earlier book[1] we explained why this suggestion is both self-contradictory and unworkable, and will not repeat the issues here. Sufficient to say that the claim of Christianity is that its central teachings are 'true' not just for *some* people, but in an objective sense. It is *the* truth about God and Jesus, not just *one* truth amongst many diverging or conflicting truths on the subject.

So how do we *know* that it's true? More properly (since *absolute* certainty about *anything* in this life is – philosophically speaking – impossible), what is the *evidence* that gives us good reason to believe that it's true? That's what this book is about.

Who's it for?

The book is aimed at anyone, whether committed Christian or not, who wants to think seriously about the subject. It is not intended to be 'academic', but to have an easy style. Obviously, deep questions cannot always be answered simply – and some readers may have to learn terms not previously known to them. We believe, however, that it should be possible to write in an easy, brief style without sacrificing a determination to present only what is factual and checkable. Footnotes have been added mainly to demonstrate the checkability of the statements made.

---

[1] *That's A Good Question* (1977), Appendix.

Structure

After the introductory chapter: 'Why bother about God?' the book gives the main positive reasons for accepting Christianity as the most likely explanation of human observation and experience. The final chapter, 'Over to you!' is a challenge to the reader to respond.

The authors

Roger T Forster has an MA in theology and mathematics from Cambridge University. He is the leader of the Ichthus Christian Fellowship in London, and is known internationally as a preacher, speaker and evangelical leader. He is a member of the Council for the Evangelical Alliance, Vice President of TEAR Fund, and Administrator and founder of the March for Jesus movement.

V Paul Marston has a BSc(Econ) and an MSc in statistical theory from the London School of Economics, an MSc in the history and philosophy of science, and a PhD which concerned science, methodology and Christian faith. He is a Senior Lecturer in the University of Central Lancashire, where his lecturing includes courses on science/religion issues.

Both authors share an evangelical viewpoint which they hope is thoughtful!

2

Why bother about God?

"It's his day off!"

Religion – Ugh!

'Religion is boring!' 'Religion is negative!' 'Religious people are often narrow and hypocritical!' People sometimes say things like that. But Jesus and his early followers were actually very critical of 'religion'. In fact, some of Jesus's most severe criticisms were made of people who were highly religious. He called them hypocrites and they became his sworn enemies.[2] The word 'religion' itself is used in the New Testament only by St Paul, who says he used to be religious

---

[2] See, e.g. Matthew 23

before he became a Christian,[3] and by St James, who criticises showy ceremonial religion and says *real* religious practices should be personal purity and acts of love towards hurt and disadvantaged people.[4]

Some religious people may well be bizarre, narrow, or hypocritical. But we are concerned here with some questions which are more fundamental than religious practices or signing up for particular creeds. Our concern is about whether or not there is a personal Creator-God, and how he or she relates to us.

God's existence – what's at stake

Let us be clear on what is involved in this. The question of the existence or non-existence of God is not the same as, for example, the existence or non-existence of 'Big Foot'.[5] Whether 'Big Foot' exists (or not) is all very interesting, but it doesn't really affect our lives at all. The existence or non-existence of a personal Creator-God, in contrast, is vitally connected with four basic issues which concern each one of us:

● *Purpose:* If God planned and created the universe, it has purpose, but if not then it is presumably just a big accident, unplanned and pointless.

● *Personhood:* If we were designed by a personal God, then there is a special meaning to being a 'person'. If there is no God, then we must be no more than the accidental side-product of purely random movements of physical atoms. Our 'personhood' would then be at best an accident and in some senses a delusion.

---

[3] Acts 26:5

[4] James 1:26-27

[5] 'Big Foot' is the American version of the 'Abominable Snowman' or 'Yeti', a half-human giant supposed to live around the Himalayan snow-line

● *Morality:* Morality hinges upon the fact that we are personal beings. But if there is no God then (as already mentioned) personal beings must be accidental and without especial significance. In this case how can there be a real meaning or value in words like 'right' and 'wrong'? Why should they apply to us any more than to any other accidentally evolved animal? For mutual selfish benefit we might agree not to harm each other, but there can be no meaning to terms like 'human right' or 'justice' beyond agreed mutual convenience.

● *Future:* If there is no God and we are accidental by-products of a blind physical universe, then there is no ultimate future for us either as individuals or as a species. Our individual conscious experience will end in death, and life on our planet will end when the sun expands – if we haven't already blown ourselves up by then.

None of this, of course, *proves* that there is a God. But what it shows is that the question itself is important to each one of us.

Evidence

3

What is the evidence for God?

"Now, Miss Simpkins, we like our staff to write any
reports and conclusions before looking at the
evidence, so that they don't get confused by the facts."

Lines of evidence

We suggest three basic lines of evidence which, taken
together, convince us that Christianity is a true picture
of reality:

● *Nature:* The modern scientific picture of our physical
universe seems to cry out that it was designed and is not
'self-sufficient'.

● *History:* If there is a personal God, we must wonder if he
or she has communicated with humankind. The historical Jesus
is a key figure for the three main one-God religions: Judaism,
Islam and Christianity. The picture of Jesus in the New

Testament fits coherently into a whole-Bible pattern, and seems also to be confirmed by historical evidence.

● *Experience:* All human beings have experience of consciousness, many witness the miraculous, and any who are Christians may have spiritual, God-focused experiences too. Each is a strand of evidence for the truth of the Christian view of reality.

Are all three lines of evidence important?

Sometimes one meets Christians who claim that some particular piece of personal religious experience is alone a sufficient and final proof of Christianity. This is misguided. Personal experience of the Holy Spirit is important, but *on its own* it can later be doubted or 'reinterpreted' as some kind of self-induced psychological delusion.

Christianity is a historical faith relating to a Creator-God; it is not just a subjective experience. The Apostle Paul had profound personal religious experiences, starting with his famous vision of a light and the voice of Jesus which led to his conversion.[6] But he also said:

> what may be known about God is plain' because 'since the creation of the world God's invisible qualities – his eternal power and divine nature – have been clearly seen, being understood from what has been made....[7]

This was an appeal to deduction from nature. Then, writing to Christians about the resurrection of Jesus, Paul appeals not to their own subjective experience but to the known historical

---

[6] Acts 9:3-7
[7] Romans 1:19-20

evidence about the resurrection appearances.[8] This was an appeal to history. Experience, nature and history – Paul regarded as important all the three strands of evidence we have identified in this chapter.

Evidence and belief-system

Each of us looks at 'evidence' with a prior 'belief-system' about the nature of reality. There are some major divisions of belief-system. One (called 'physicalism') is that there is no reality outside the strictly physical. A second is that there is some type of dimension or realm of 'persons' or 'mind', but no personal Creator-God. A third major category in belief-systems (and this includes Christianity) is that the physical is related to and maintained in existence by a personal God who can vary the patterns which happen in it if he or she[9] so chooses.

All belief-systems become adept at 'explaining away' bits of apparent counter-evidence – so we cannot hope to present an *individual* piece of 'evidence' to conclusively 'prove' the truth of our own views. Someone who is determined (for example) to accept no reality but the physical can explain away anything we may present. What we *would* argue is simply that the Christian view makes overall the most coherent sense of reality and of human experiences of it.

Making sense without making trite

Christianity is committed to considering and meeting reasonable questions and objections. The apostle Paul wrote:

---

[8] 1 Corinthians 15:3-8

[9] Whilst such a Creator would have no gender in the strict sense, and whilst 'political corrrectness' may be desirable, we will henceforth refer to God conventionally with the less cumbersome 'he'

We demolish arguments and every pretension that sets itself up against the knowledge of God, and we take captive every thought to make it obedient to Christ.[10]

As we have seen, Paul himself, whilst he focused on the central issue of the importance of faith, strongly believed Christianity to be objectively and historically true. 'Taking every thought captive' does not mean mindlessness, but thinking through the truth and relating it to Christian belief.

In this we must always be honest. Whilst we believe Christianity makes the most 'sense', this does not mean that it has no problems or questions. However, this is true of all knowledge. There are, for example, outstanding problems and puzzles in physics – but this doesn't stop us accepting and using the bits we do understand. In this book we want to present the evidence, but we don't want to be glib. Various problems do need considering,[11] but this should not stop us responding to the positive evidence. There are also 'mysteries' which are beyond human thought and language, but this should not stop us using human thought and language to understand as much as we may.

---

[10] 2 Corinthians 10:5
[11] We have done so in our earlier book *Reason and Faith*, and intend further publications on problem issues

4

Science: assertions and limits

"Of course this does simplify it a bit!"

The basic question

Certain experiences are common to humans throughout history:

● A conscious use of *language* to represent the structure and relationships of the physical world.[12]

● An experience of 'purpose' – of acting (i.e. changing the

---

[12] This is classically analysed by the philosopher Karl Popper and the medical brain expert John Eccles in *The Self and Its Brain* (1977). Genesis 2:19-20 also emphasises a uniquely human use of *conceptual* language

physical world) by plan. To 'create' a new kitchen, for example, means *planning* it in one's mind before it exists in the physical world.

● An awareness that physical reality seems to follow patterns or 'laws', and a concern as to whether these patterns are purely accidental or are a result of the plan/design of a personal Creator.

Of this last and central question there have always been two views. The Epicureans, who disputed with Paul in Athens,[13] believed neither in a Creator-God, nor that the universe was designed. They claimed that everything was due to an unplanned and unintended fortuitous or chance association of atoms following physical laws. Speaking of this, Minucius Felix, an early third-century Christian, wrote:

> I feel the more convinced that people who hold this universe of consummate artistic beauty to be not the work of divine planning, but a conglomeration of some kind of fragments clinging together by chance, are themselves devoid of reason and perception.[14]

As science developed, the same basic choice remained – is the physical world planned or accidental? Robert Boyle, a key early scientist and a founder of the Royal Society, wrote of

> some, whose partiality for chance makes them willing to ascribe the structures of animals to that, rather than to a designing cause.[15]

Was the universe designed or was it accidental and purposeless? The choice has always been there. Modern atheists, who believe it is purposeless, are unoriginal.

---

[13] Acts 17:18

[14] Minucius Felix, *Dialogue* (*c*. AD 220)

[15] Robert Boyle, *A Disquisition...* (1688), p. 525

What science says on origins

So how exactly does modern science fit into the argument? The typical picture of 'origins' in any university science faculty (and remember that one of the present authors works in one) would run something like this:

● Between 8-18 billion[16] years ago our universe (including its time and space) began with a 'big bang' – giving rise to a universe which has been expanding ever since.

● The matter arising from the big bang began to undergo a complex process in which stars and galaxies formed and developed in predictable ways.

● Our solar system formed some 4-5 billion years ago (the Earth about 4.6 billion) by mechanisms still under dispute.

● Life began with tiny micro-organisms 3.5-4 billion years ago. Multicellular animals began around 700 million years ago. Land colonisation began some 425 million years ago.

● Varieties of living creatures evolved. Mutations in genetic codes (DNA) were occasionally beneficial and enabled the animals bearing those mutated genes better to survive and pass the genes on. This process of 'natural selection' led to accumulated changes and a divergence of life forms increasingly specialised to fit particular niches in a natural environment itself subject to change. This process is broadly reflected in the sequence of fossils in the geological strata.

● Mankind evolved, probably through a fairly narrow 'bottleneck' in geologically recent time, with modern man appearing sometime in the last 100,000 years.

Now there are some Christians who would question not merely details of this but the whole thing. We consider this

---

[16] Apparent agreement on 13-18 billion years has been challenged by measurements from the Hubble space telescope, see: *Nature*, 371, 27 October 1994 pp. 757-61

'radical critique' elsewhere,[17] but let us suppose for the present that we accept this scientific description of the physical world as more or less accurate as far as it goes. In saying this, of course, we need to note:

1. This kind of view is taught in science faculties both by Christians and non-Christians (though they may differ in their views of whether it was designed or accidental and Christians usually see the creation of humankind in a special light).

2. No scientific law is known with certainty, and in the past laws have been replaced or been seen to be special cases. Current science claims to embody the best presently available hypotheses to explain observations.

3. There are a number of problems or anomalies in current theories, which may result in minor or radical revision.

4. Timescale estimates depend on assumptions, and may prove inaccurate – a reduction of 13-18 to 8 billion years has been suggested just recently! It must, however, be added that whilst we might imagine some further reduction due to new evidence to (say) 3-4 billion, a reduction to (say) 6,000 years would be so fundamental as to be almost inconceivable to most present scientists.

But if this broad scientific picture is accepted , what then?

The limits of science

Firstly, science is limited in its subject area. Albert Einstein, perhaps the most revered scientist of the twentieth century, wrote:

> The scientific method can teach us nothing beyond how facts are related to and conditioned by each other... knowledge of what is does not open the door directly to what should be. One can have the

---

[17]E.g. in our book *Reason and Faith*

clearest and most complete knowledge of what *is*, and yet not be able to deduce from that what should be the *goal* of our human aspirations...[18]

Professor Stephen Hawking, author of the best selling book *A Brief History of Time* and one of the best-known present scientists, wrote:

...even if there is only one unique set of possible laws, it is only a set of equations. What is it that breathes fire into the equations and makes a universe for them to govern?... Although science may solve the problem of how the universe began, it cannot answer the question: why does the universe bother to exist? I don't know the answer to that. [19]

Scientific observation can tell us, for example, about:
● atoms and molecules (physics and chemistry)
● mechanisms of living things (biology)
● rocks and the structure and dynamics of the earth (geology)
● human behaviour and thinking (sociology and psychology)

But it cannot tell us about right, wrong, purpose and meaning. This is not because it 'hasn't progressed far enough yet'. It is because such issues are simply not its subject-matter.

It is, of course, possible to argue that the *only* valid kind of explanation is the scientific one, and that all other kinds are meaningless. This is a view which restricts reality.

Interestingly, philosophers of the 'logical positivist' school (*c*.1926-70) went even further, and restricted reality to the directly observable! They suggested that any statement which was not provable by direct observation was meaningless – i.e.

[18] Albert Einstein, *Ideas and Opinions* (1954, repr. 1973), p. 41
[19] Stephen Hawking, *Black Holes and Baby Universes* (1993), p. 90

was not really a statement at all. By the late 1970s, however, it was transparently obvious that logical positivism was hopelessly unworkable, and even its leading British advocate repudiated it.[20]   Human experience was too rich and too 'subjective' for such a philosophy to work.

Someone who still repeatedly suggests that *only* scientific explanations are meaningful is the scientist Richard Dawkins.[21] Perhaps we should not expect too much from those like Dawkins and Peter Atkins who are after all scientists not philosophers,[22] but we must insist that science be kept in philosophical perspective. A commitment to science should imply neither 'scientism' (a belief that science has all the answers) nor 'physicalism' (a belief that nothing except the physical world is real). The suggestion that the physical world is *all* that exists is a possible but (to most of us) an implausible one. To accept it would mean denying effective reality to so much of our individual experience (right, wrong, personal volition etc.). The *physicalist* lives in a narrow and impoverished reality.

We have also to recognise that a physical description of mechanism does not, in itself, tell us whether any person planned for the events to happen. In the view of Jesus, it was God who fed the birds.[23]   This did not, of course, mean that Jesus believed God specially created worms each morning. The

---

[20] Long-time leading positivist Professor A J Ayer, in an interview in *The Listener*, 2nd March 1978, said 'nearly all of it was false'

[21] An excellent analysis of Dawkins is given by Michael Poole in *Science and Christian Belief*, 6 (1), April 1994, pp. 41-59

[22] We note Kelly J Clark, in *Philosophers Who Believe* (1993), p. 9, says at least 1,000 practising academic professional philosophers now reckon themselves as Christians. Keith Ward in *The Turn of the Tide* (1988) makes a similar point

[23] Matthew 6:26

food of birds is produced by the regular cycles of nature – which biologists can study and understand in more and more detail. But no amount of mechanical detail can, in itself, tell us whether the whole process existed in the mind and plan of God before it came to exist in the physical world. The mechanism and the purpose are two different issues.

Most of us, then, recognise that the subject matter of science, however successful, is only part of reality. For meaning, plan and purpose, we need to look elsewhere.

5

Science, origins and chance

"We hope he comes out with a tea set."

A chancy business

The word 'chance' is used in at least two very distinct senses:

1. *Chance₁=probability:* This sense of 'chance' concerns statistical patterns. Given a set of possible outcomes to some situation, statistics {Chance₁=Probability} tells us what proportion of them have a particular feature.

> E.g. The chance of an ace being drawn from a pack of cards is $\frac{4}{52}$ or 7.7%. (odds = 12:1)

2. *Chance$_2$=undesigned:* In this sense a 'chance' event is one that no-one planned or intended.

> E.g. 'John and Mary met by chance' implies that no-one planned for the event to happen

These senses *are* distinct. One relates to the mathematical properties of sets, whilst the other relates to the presence or absence of a personal agent and design. One is properly used within the subject-matter of physical science, the other is not. Since the differences *are* so vital, we hope that readers will bear with our rather cumbersome differentiation between {chance$_1$=probability} and {chance$_2$=undesigned} in what follows.

Relating different senses of 'chance'

There are important ways in which the two senses of 'chance' relate.

Firstly, the use of probability theory {chance$_1$=probability} to describe phenomena does not imply that they are 'chance' {chance$_2$=undesigned} in the second sense. Take suicides. Statisticians know that numbers of suicides fit a probability pattern known as the 'Poisson distribution'. But this is not to deny that each individual act of suicide involved someone in what was very much a personal act of design and decision. Suicide is a 'chance' {chance$_1$=probability} event in the first sense but certainly not in the {chance$_2$=undesigned} second.

Scientists do sometimes confuse the two. In a famous book Jacques Monod describes statistically the various mutations which can occur in genetics, and then adds: 'We say that these events are accidental, due to chance... chance alone is the source of every innovation...'[24] He switches from issues of

---

[24] Jaques Monod, *Chance and Necessity* (1970), p. 110

statistics {chance$_1$=probability} to issues of purpose {chance$_2$=undesigned}. He is, of course, as entitled to his atheistic view as the Christian geneticist who may believe in a purpose behind it all – but he should not confuse the two types of 'chance'.

It should be noted that 'chance' {chance$_2$=undesigned} is not an alternative agent to God, but an assertion that there is no agent or design at all. We can, of course, easily be mistaken in jumping to the conclusion that an event is 'chance' {chance$_2$=undesigned}, when actually someone has planned it. In the example above, it may turn out that John 'happening to meet' Mary looked unplanned, but in fact Cynthia had been plotting for weeks to bring them together! We should beware when some people urge us to jump to the conclusion that parts of the universe look 'unplanned' and are therefore 'chance' in this sense {chance$_2$=undesigned}.

'Chance', coincidence and design

There is another way in which the two senses of 'chance' relate. Here is a demonstration done for students by one of us (guess which one!):

Three packs of cards were produced, each one containing two blanks, three O's, and one each of the letters D, E, G, L, S, U, V and Y.

Each pack was shuffled by a different student and taken back by the lecturer, who laid each pack out by turning over each card in turn on a table. The three packs looked like this:

Pack 1:	E	D	G	V	O	O		L	S	O		U	Y
Pack 2:	S	D	U	G	V	L	E		O	Y		O	O
Pack 3:	G	O	D		L	O	V	E	S		Y	O	U

Now there are actually 518,918,400 distinct possible orders in which these cards could come up. The first two patterns passed without comment, but the third brought howls of disbelief! All three patterns *might,* of course, have been deliberately engineered by the lecturer – but in any event the students were sure about the third one.

The 'chances' {chance$_1$=probability} of getting a meaningful pattern by 'chance' {chance$_2$=undesigned} would be remote.

'Coincidence' seemed implausible.

Conclusion: someone planned it!

PS: Watch out Paul Daniels and David Copperfield!

'Chance', 'chances' and origins

There are some basic points at which similar logic can apply to present scientific theories about origins.

We are presently going to ask three questions:

(1) Why does the structure of matter enable inhabitable universes to form?

(2) Why is *this* universe inhabitable?

(3) How did life actually originate?

Of these, (1) concerns fundamental physical constants, where there are amazing 'coincidences' which enable the conditions to be formed for life. Regarding (2) and (3), let's consider the implications of two possibilities:

● Suppose that it were possible to show that, given suitable basic physical constants, there would be good 'chances' {chance$_1$=probability} in the course of a nature based on those constants, of getting first an inhabitable universe and then the formation of life. This would *not* necessarily imply that these events were 'chance' {chance$_2$=undesigned}. As already indicated, we believe that God works through natural processes, and they are not independent of him. He could well have set natural physical constants which led naturally to life.

● Suppose, on the other hand, it turns out that (even given suitable basic physical constants as in (1)) the 'chances' {chance$_1$=probability} of getting first an inhabitable universe and then a formation of life are actually pretty remote. This would then give much stronger evidence that it was not {chance$_2$=undesigned} but someone planned it.

There is a direct parallel here with the card demonstration above. The first two sequences of letters *might have been* planned by the lecturer, whereas the students were *sure* that the third had been planned. The 'improbable' pattern in the third made much stronger the evidence that it had been planned.

With this in mind we may now ask the three questions:

(1) Why does the structure of matter enable inhabitable universes to form?

Various fundamental physical constants seem to be very 'fine tuned' to allow the formation of chemical elements as we know them. Elements essential to life – like carbon – are 'manufactured' inside stars from lighter elements. Very, very precise 'coincidences' of energy levels in helium-4, beryllium-8, carbon-12, and oxygen-16 are needed for carbon to form without it all turning into oxygen. Cambridge Professor of Astronomy Martin Rees and popular science writer John Gribbin state:

> This combination of coincidences, just right for resonance in carbon-12, just wrong in oxygen-16, is indeed remarkable. There is no better evidence to support the argument that the Universe has been designed for our benefit – tailor made for man.'[25]

[25] John Gribbin and Martin Rees, *Cosmic Coincidences* (1990), p. 247

Though they themselves reject the conclusion that there was a Creator, Rees and Gribbin go on to mention that there are: 'at least two other striking coincidences that help to make the Universe a fit place for life.' Thus, for example, if one of the four fundamental forces in nature (weak interaction) had been very, very slightly different, then the stellar production and distribution of essential heavier elements could not have taken place.[26] In this case we could not have been here.

(2) Why is this universe inhabitable?

Even given suitable fundamental constants, a 'big bang' along the lines of present scientific theory could have produced a great number of different universes. The vastly overwhelming proportion of these would be (in crude terms) either a series of black holes or have matter spread out thinly and evenly. In none of these could life exist.

We need to get an idea of the numbers involved here.

Professor Paul Davies is a physicist, a popular writer on both sides of the Atlantic, and has no Christian axe to grind. He has estimated that for every time a big bang produced a universe in which life could exist, there would be one followed by at least a thousand billion billion billion zeros of universes where life was impossible.[27]   There would be astronomical odds against getting a universe where life was possible.

How then should we explain the fact that we are in a universe

---

[26] John Gribbin and Martin Rees, *Cosmic Coincidences* (1990), pp. 252-4

[27] These figures are in Paul Davies, *Other Worlds* (1980), p. 168, since when some scientists have suggested that a suitable 'inflationary model' may, if demonstrated, reduce the odds. Davies himself (though unconvinced of a Creator-God) still notes numbers of wildly 'improbable' design features in the later *The Mind of God* (1992)

where life *is* possible? One obvious answer would be 'someone planned it' – like the card example above. But suppose, for the moment, we try to find an answer which leaves it unplanned and accidental. Some have tried to argue like this:

> Since it is inhabitable, it must have happened. However improbable it seems, now that we know that it is inhabitable we have to accept that the unlikely odd did in fact come up.

This is not very plausible. It was tried with the students in the card experiment without success. 'Look,' the lecturer argued, 'since you now know that it did in fact happen to come up, you have to accept that it *did* happen by 'chance' {chance$_2$=undesigned} whatever the odds against.' They weren't convinced. The issue was not whether or not the cards came up meaningfully (we all knew that they had), but whether or not someone planned it.

Another attempt to avoid a divine planner for the universe runs like this.

> Suppose that there are actually an enormous number of universes, all started by unplanned big bangs. Just occasionally one will arise in which life is possible. Obviously, it is *that* one in which we would evolve and be here to ask questions about origins! So here we are!

This sounds a bit more plausible, and some reputable physicists have suggested multiple universe models. But what evidence is there that there are *in fact* a large number of alternative universes? None at all. It all looks like a pretty desperate attempt to avoid a belief in a creator.

(3) How did life actually originate?

Supposing that a big bang produced a universe in which life was possible. Suppose also that, amongst the myriads of planets which we presume (although we cannot presently check) are scattered throughout it, some happened to have the very, very narrow conditions needed for life to exist. What would be needed for life to begin, and how often would it come about by 'chance' {$chance_1$=probability} if not designed?

Life implies reproduction. This must involve genetic information being used (with a suitable energy source) to build living structures from basic chemical building blocks and also pass on its own genetic or replication code.

The basic building blocks for life are:
- amino-acids to build proteins
- nucleotides for nucleic acids (RNA or DNA)
- monosacchrides (single sugars) and lipids

HEALTH WARNING: those who've studied biology will find the next few paragraphs easy if not simplistic, some other readers may find their brains beginning to hurt!

Vast numbers of 'building blocks' are involved. The human cell, for example, contains 46 chromosomes (molecules of DNA) totalling some 6 billion bonded pairs of nucleotides (adenine-thymine, and guanine-cytosine pairings) the order of which contains the human genetic code. The 'simple' *E. coli* bacterium (living in our gut!) is a 'prokaryotic' single cell (i.e. has no nucleus), but has a wound-up DNA strand which is 1,000 times its own length and has 3,000 genes made of some 4 million base pairs. RNA is a shorter, usually single-stranded molecule, but still with large numbers of nucleotide bases. Even proteins may have molecular weights of 50,000.

The whole is part of a complex, interdependent cycle. All living cells today are either eukaryotic or prokaryotic. The eukaryotes contain DNA strands in a nucleus, the simpler prokaryotes (bacteria) contain DNA strands but have no nucleus. In both types, part of the DNA information is copied onto smaller transient messenger RNA (mRNA) molecules.

These then (having, in eukaryotic cells, passed through pores in the nuclear envelope into the cytoplasm) interact with the transfer RNA (tRNA) molecules and with ribosomes to translate the information in the mRNA and form long chains of correctly sequenced amino acids to make proteins. During all this the cell has to perform many other metabolic processes (e.g. respiration), requiring gene expression. The DNA also replicates itself by unwinding, splitting along its 'ladder-like' structure of bonded pairs of nucleotides, and each of the millions of nucleotides along each half attracting and bonding with an appropriate available nucleotide (synthesised by the cell itself) to form two new complete DNA strands.

DNA therefore has two fundamental properties which are required by any genetic material: it can self-replicate and it can direct a chain of syntheses which produce the proteins, required for all cellular properties, including the synthesis of the nucleotide building blocks needed for replication.

Sound complicated ? Brain hurting ? It's horrendous!

Note that there's a serious 'chicken and egg' problem here. Proteins cannot be synthesised without DNA (or RNA), but you cannot make DNA without proteins to act as catalysts to synthesise the building blocks of DNA.

Even the most ardent atheist recognises that the chances of getting just one DNA molecule (let alone an ongoing system) merely by random movements of atoms, are much less than those of accidentally assembling a jumbo jet by an explosion in the parts factory!

Any 'non-miraculous' model for life origins must therefore be based on the idea of the DNA molecule 'evolving' rather than spontaneously forming. Such a model must explain:

1. How did the basic organic building blocks originate in adequate quantities and proportions?

2. How did some of these come together to form more complex organic molecules which 'locked on' rather than

simply fall apart again or be broken down by other chemical agents present?

3. How did they survive and begin to replicate, with all the complex interdependence of even the simplest system?

Hearing some enthusiastic popular scientists one might get the impression that such a process of molecular evolution was unproblematic Actually there are massive problems at every major stage of it. Experiments with electrical discharge in gaseous soup (begun in the 1950s) produce only unconcentrated organic building blocks, mostly in minute quantities. How and where could they become concentrated in the early earth? How could they eventually build into ongoing 'simple' life systems with all their complexities?

The most popular speculation today is that life originated with RNA. All modern cells (even bacteria) use DNA for genetic code, and use RNA only as a kind of messenger. The 'flexibility' of RNA is, however, shown in that it has forms (ribozymes) which can act instead of protein as a catalyst, and it can form the genetic basis of some viruses[28] – occasionally as a double rather than single chain. The problem is that it is less stable and, in its normal single strand form, cannot reproduce itself by dividing and attracting opposite bases. So it is speculated that this early RNA replicated 'abiotically' (i.e. in a non-living way), perhaps held for stability on clay surfaces. Laboratories, carefully adjusting suitable extreme conditions and quantities of suitable building blocks, can get very short RNA-like structures to replicate. Other scientists are sceptical of the possibility of such a purely 'RNA world': no such system now exists anywhere, and no real molecular details of how such a system could be viable are forthcoming.

---

[28] A virus, of course, is not itself a living cell, and can replicate only by using the facilities of a living host cell. Viruses could not, therefore, have been the first 'life'

In the 1950s life was thought relatively simple, and Miller's synthesis of basic organic 'building blocks' a major step towards explaining its origins. It turned out to be a horrendously complicated, very interdependent system, and to many, the 1950s optimism now looks rather naive.

One might expect scepticism from some of the Christian biologists and geologists not committed to the inevitability of a purely 'naturalistic' explanation.[29] But, perhaps more notably, in a chapter on 'origins of cellular life', Stephen L Wolfe's standard advanced textbook[30] states that once the basic building blocks :

> ... formed in sufficient quantities, they presumably assembled spontaneously into macromolecules such as proteins and nucleic acids. A major problem presented by such assembly reaction is that they primarily involve chemical condensations... it is not clear how condensations became predominant in the primitive environment. (p. 1127)

Formation in the sea, underwater volcanoes, and hot clays (as mentioned, the current hot favourite!) have all been suggested – and all have problems. Wolfe goes on to admit:

> ...the specific reactions accomplishing the transformation of non-living to living matter have proved to be the most difficult to imagine and test... (p. 1132)

At the end of his long discussion, and before an impressive looking up-to-date 'further reading', Wolfe states:

---

[29] E.g. L R Croft, *How Life Began* (1988), or Jim Brooks, *Origins of Life* (1985)

[30] Stephen L Wolfe, *Molecular and Cellular Biology* (1993)

'The events outlined in this chapter, leading from the earth's origins to the appearance of eukaryotic cells, are admittedly hypothetical and so tenuous that they may seem impossible. But given the total time span of these events, 3.5 billion years, the impossible becomes possible, the possible probable, and the probable virtually certain...' (p. 1142)

This 'time achieves anything' argument (due originally to Wald) seems pretty desperate. Compared with developing eukaryotic cells, problems involved in getting pigs to fly pale into insignificance!

Another modern standard (undergraduate) text admits:

The origin of life remains a matter of scientific speculation, and there are alternative views of how several key processes occurred... Whatever way prebiotic chemicals accumulated, polymerised, and eventually reproduced, the leap from an aggregate of molecules that reproduces to even the simplest prokaryotic cell is immense and must have been taken in many smaller evolutionary steps...[31]

These steps must have taken less than 1 billion years after the earth formed (by Wolfe's figures less than a half billion years after earth conditions became suitable). No detailed natural molecular mechanisms for them are suggested or available.

The standard texts are littered with 'may haves', 'must haves' 'conceivablys' and 'presumablys'; but mechanisms are speculative rather than detailed.

Even the journal *Nature* itself, pursuing what it calls its 'reductionists' agenda, of removing purpose from explanation, admits that after an extensive post-war search for possible 'natural' mechanisms for life origins:

Unfortunately, there is as yet not much that is tangible to

---

[31] Neil A Campbell, *Biology* (3rd edition, 1993), p. 511

report...there have been many pointed investigations... but there is not yet an unambiguous pointer to the mechanisms that may have led to the emergence of living organisms... [32]

The search for a 'natural' evolving-molecule model for the origins of life remains, of course, a valid part of scientific research programmes. Some suitable mechanistic explanation *may*, one day, be forthcoming. Conceivably someone *may*, one day, invent a model which explains in detail how each stage of the increasingly complex molecular structures 'locked on', until the final stage of a replicating life system was reached. But if we stick with what science there actually is now rather than wishful thinking or scientific 'triumphalism', then it has to be said that there is nothing at present which even gets close.

So where does all this leave us?

Christians are *not*, of course, saying that 'God' is introduced only to fill in missing bits in our understanding. This approach, sometimes called 'god of the gaps' thinking, is mistaken. God is the author of all of nature, not merely someone who occasionally 'interferes' in bits of it. Even if (and it's a big 'if') one day there are convincing mechanical explanations with high probability for all the past series of physical events, still it would be pretty amazing and still questions about 'why' and purpose would remain. But it has also to be said that, at present, *according to existing scientific theories:*

● Fundamental physical constants contain a number of really amazing 'coincidences' which enable chemical elements to be generated.

● It would be *wildly* improbable that a big bang would produce a universe in which life could exist.

---

[32] *Nature*, 3 November 1994, p. 29

● Even if planets are common, not many would have the narrow conditions required for life.

● For molecular evolution leading to life, there is no present detailed model which avoids fairly wild improbability.

Think of the card experiment.

What is the reasonable conclusion? Did the words 'GOD LOVES YOU' form accidentally – or did someone plan it? Did a big bang accidentally lead to an inhabitable universe in which life accidentally developed – or did someone plan it?

Is 'God' a real explanation?

Finally, some have argued that for us to use 'God' to explain why the universe is as it is just adds another level of mystery, i.e. 'Why is God as he is?' They argue that it is 'simpler' just to accept the universe as a 'brute fact' rather than to add another thing to be explained as well.[33] The fallacy with their argument is that we are not adding a new and unexperienced 'thing' to explain. Actually, our most direct experience (see below, Chapter 11) is of ourselves being personal beings – so to suggest that a personal being created an inhabitable world is not to add to the number of things requiring explanation. In a sense, it reduces it from two things requiring explanation (i.e. personhood and an inhabitable universe) to one (personhood) which through Creation explains both the physical universe and the existence of ourselves as persons.

A Creator-God makes sense of *all* our experience of reality.

---

[33] Paul Davies reproduces this argument in *The Mind of God*, p. 59

6

Has God been in touch?

"We thought we might as well update it a bit whilst we were at it."

Creation and communication

Suppose that our universe, life, and us, are not accidental by-products of blind processes, but rather are a result of a plan made by a *person* having a mind.

We can understand this idea only because of its parallels with our own experience of being persons who plan things. But we must always remember our limitations. Any being who planned and created something like our universe must surely be something rather more than a big version of us. We have, however, no choice but to try to understand God in terms we can relate to (which may involve picture language, analogy, etc.).

This is no different from, say, sub-atomic physics, which sometimes we struggle to understand in terms and picture language to which we can relate. Terms like 'particles', 'streams', and 'waves' in such physics are partial pictures, not 'literal' ones. Profound reality is not simple, it is not always 'imaginable', and our language is limited in describing it.

With this caution in mind, though, it still seems rational to ask: 'Would such a personal God, who made the universe, living things and people wish to communicate with them?' Surely, yes. So are there any claims to be communications from him?

Actually, there aren't many.

Religions like animism concern the day-by-day placating of innumerable spirits and, although they may have a 'high god' or 'great spirit', they offer little information about him.

Other major religions are what we call 'religions of the way'. There are, of course, great differences between the respective 'ways' of Hinduism (Dharma), Buddhism (the Eightfold path) and Taoism (Tao). In Hinduism, for example, the Bhagavad-Gita emphasises a devotion to deities which is foreign to the others. What they share is a lack of emphasis on the personhood of the individual – and parallel to this, a lack of strong identity of a personal Creator-God. The individual seeks not right-standing before a personal and righteous God, but 'enlightenment', implying either personal extinction or absorption into some kind of universal. None of these religions contains claims to communication from a personal Creator-God.

The three major faiths which *do* make such a claim are Judaism, Christianity and Islam. So what about them? One of the most immediately striking things is that the man Jesus of Nazareth is associated in a vital way with all three! Assessing the claims of the various sacred writings to be from God, we therefore have to ask this central question:

Who was Jesus?

There have, in fact, been lots of very bizarre suggestions about Jesus in recent years. An early one (not by any kind of scholar – but still available in high-street shops) hints at him being a space visitor![34] But apparent 'scholars' can also be eccentric. One claimed it was all to do with 'magic mushrooms',[35] another that Jesus was 'really' a twice-married, long-lived family man,[36] whilst another recently claimed (on extraordinarily obscure linguistic grounds) that 'really' Jesus was not crucified but was stoned by a Jewish court.[37] Because they are 'sensational', such books tend to be the ones stocked by big high-street bookshops, but they inevitably involve ignoring whole masses of solid evidence whilst building castles in the air on some tiny obscure point. They are a bit like suggesting that Margaret Thatcher was 'really' a left-wing Wicked Witch of the West because she once wore red shoes!

Let's leave the bizarre.

Three views of Jesus

Three serious alternative views of Jesus actually relate to the three main 'one-God' faiths: Judaism, Christianity, and Islam, the relationships between which are complex.

Jesus and the earliest Christians were, of course, Jews, and there are many Jews today who are Christians and believe that Jesus was the Jewish Messiah. Christians see their faith as a completion and fulfilment of pre-Christian Jewish faith. However, the non-Christian Judaism which is reflected in the Jewish Mishnah (compiled about AD 100 and AD 200) and the

---

[34] Erich Von Daniken, *Chariots of the Gods* (1967)

[35] John Allegro, *The Sacred Mushroom and the Cross* (1973)

[36] Barbara Thiering, *Jesus the Man* (1992)

[37] Enoch Powell, *The Evolution of the Gospel* (1994)

later Talmud, accepted Jesus as neither prophet nor Messiah. This means that, with the Muslim view, there are three different and irreconcilable views of who Jesus was:

1. A Jewish Magician: The Jewish Talmud presents Jesus as an executed 'sorcerer'.

Jesus was hanged on the Passover Eve. Forty days previously the herald had cried, 'He is being led out for stoning, because he practised sorcery and led Israel astray and enticed them into apostasy. Whoever has anything to say in his defence, let him come and declare it.' As nothing was brought forward in his defence he was hanged on Passover Eve.[38]

Some modern books also present him as basically a Jewish wonder-worker, misunderstood and deified by later followers.[39]

2. The Son of God: The New Testament presents Jesus as a human Jewish prophet but also identifies him as the divine 'Word become flesh',[40] who died for human sin and was resurrected to bring eternal life:

Just as Moses lifted up the snake in the desert, so the Son of Man [Jesus] must be lifted up [in crucifixion] so that everyone who believes in him may have eternal life. For God so loved the world that he gave his one and only Son, that whoever believes in him shall not perish but have eternal life.[41]

---

[38] *Babylonian Sanhedrin* 43a
[39] E.g. Geza Vermes, *Jesus the Jew* (1983); Morton Smith, *Jesus the Magician* (1978)
[40] John 1:14
[41] John 3:16

3. A Human Prophet: The Islamic Qur'ân sees Jesus as an important prophet, not divine, and asserts of him:

> And for their saying, 'Truly we have slain the Messiah, Jesus the son of Mary, an Apostle of God.' Yet they slew him not, and they crucified him not, but they had only his likeness... but God took him up to Himself.'[42]

If Jesus did *not* die, he could not have been resurrected – a point emphasised by some Muslim writers.[43]

Christianity, Islam and non-Christian Judaism have, of course, a lot in common, but on the key question 'Who was Jesus?' they are irreconcilable. To Christians, the deity and death and resurrection of Christ are central to their faith. Non-Christian Jews may accept his crucifixion, but believe him neither divine nor a prophet. Muslims revere him as a prophet but deny both his divinity and his death.

Weighing up rival views

If, then, there is a single Creator-God who has communicated with humankind, the figure of Jesus seems central to understanding that communication. So how can the three rival views be assessed?

We will suggest two ways: coherence and correspondence. The first way is to look at the overall *coherence* of each view. We ask 'Is the Christian version of Christ a logical fulfilment of the Old Testament and its prophecy? Does it form part of a pattern which makes sense?'

---

[42] Sûrah iv.155-7

[43] In the UK, booklets by the Muslim Ahmed Deedat of the IPCI include *Crucifixion or Cruci-fiction*, etc.

The second line of approach is to look at the quality of the historical sources. Which is the best bet as a source of historical information about Jesus: the Christian New Testament, the Mishnah/Talmud of Judaism, or the Muslim Qur'ân? Does the Christian New Testament show the best *correspondence* with historical evidence?

These two issues, coherence and correspondence, form the basis of the next two chapters.

7

A pattern in God's dealings?

Unexpected agreement!

According to the Muslim holy Qur'ân, God inspired Noah and
the Jewish Old Testament prophets, 'spoke directly unto Moses'
and 'imparted unto David the Psalms'.[44] God's communication
to Moses, David and the prophets is therefore agreed by Jews,
Christians and Muslims. This 'unexpected agreement' can form a
common starting point. Christians, though, believe that this
communication 'makes sense' as forming part of a pattern into
which the New Testament Jesus fits. Is this so?

---

[44] See e.g. Sûrah v, 163-4

Much of the Old Testament concerns universal issues of right and wrong, justice, and the individual's relationship with God. But three things stand out:

1. Through Moses, God established that human sin was a serious affair, that it could not just be forgiven but needed sacrifice (pictured in animal sacrifice) to put it right.

2. From the very first, there was an indication that God's special relationship with the Jews would one day be a means for him to reach all nations.

3. There were hints of a coming 'Messiah', focused later into one who would suffer sacrificially, even die, but would be victorious.

Let's look at these three.

Sin and sacrifice

From the very beginning the God of the Bible is seen to be interested in right and wrong. In Genesis we find the account of Adam and Eve[45] and the first sin – a story repeated in the Qur'ân.[46] Soon after, a link is made between sacrifice and being accepted by God.[47]

The story of Noah is about judgement on sin,[48] and at the end of the story Noah makes a sacrifice to God.[49] Abraham, the founder and forefather of the Jewish nation, also offered sacrifice.[50]

---

[45] Discussion on how far this was intended allegorically is in our *Reason and Faith*

[46] Sûrah vii.19-25, xx.115-23

[47] Genesis 4:4. In our book *That's a Good Question*, we showed how biblical animal sacrifice was both humane and linked to a reverence for life

[48] Genesis 6:9-11 (also the Qur'ân, e.g. Sûrah xxix.14)

[49] Genesis 8:20-21

[50] Genesis 22:13

The sacrifice of the Passover lamb, begun when Israel was born as a nation, was made to turn away the divine judgement on sin.[51] With Moses, the first national Jewish leader, came a codifying of the moral law – including the 'ten commandments' – and also a clear indication of the links between sacrifice and forgiveness of sin.[52] These links were repeated throughout the history of the Jewish people, and were still there in the time of Jesus.

So what is it all about? Can sacrificing animals really, in itself, make a difference to God's forgiveness of human sin, or is it rather a picture of something deeper?

The Messiah

From the very beginning, there are growing hints that God has a plan to deal with sin – and that this centres on a coming 'Messiah' figure. A human figure who will crush the head of evil is first prophesied in Eden.[53] Later, Abraham promises: 'God will provide himself the lamb for the sacrifice.'[54]   In this Abraham surely prophesies beyond the immediate situation, and God soon afterwards promises: 'Through your offspring all nations on earth will be blessed, because you have obeyed me.'[55]

In one sense, the Old Testament pictures the nation of Israel as God's chosen servant, but in another sense there is a growing recognition that a Messiah will come to Israel.

The book of Isaiah, written some four or five centuries before Christ,[56] powerfully develops this theme. The birth of a royal child, whose titles include 'Mighty God, Everlasting Father,

---

[51] Exodus 12

[52] E.g. Leviticus 4-7; Exodus 20:1-26

[53] Genesis 3:15

[54] Genesis 22:8

[55] Genesis 22:18; see also Galatians 3:16

[56] Many scholars believe the book of Isaiah had several authors, but it was certainly one book well before the time of Christ

Prince of Peace,' is prophesied in Isaiah 9:6. The servanthood of the nation of Israel later focuses (from chapter 42) on a coming individual. Chapter 53 is worth reading in its entirety, but here is an extract:

> ... to whom has the arm of the Lord been revealed?...
> [3]He was despised and rejected by men, a man of sorrows and familiar with suffering. Like one from whom men hide their faces, he was despised and we esteemed him not. [4]Surely he took up our infirmities and carried our sorrows, yet we considered him stricken by God, smitten by him and afflicted. [5]But he was pierced for our transgressions, he was crushed for our iniquities; the punishment which brought us peace was upon him, and by his wounds we are healed. [6]We all like sheep have gone astray, each of us has turned to his own way, and the Lord has laid on him the iniquity of us all... [9]He was assigned to a grave with the wicked, and with the rich in his death, though he had done no violence, nor was any deceit in his mouth. [10]Yet it was the Lord's will to crush him and cause him to suffer, and though the Lord makes his life a guilt offering, he will see his offspring and prolong his days...

Who is this figure? He was some kind of expected Messiah, but what kind exactly? We should note:

● He is to be rejected by his fellows who will believe him judged by God (verses 3-4).

● He will be 'pierced' (verse 5) and die (verse 9).

● His death will be a sacrifice to bear others' sins and bring them forgiveness (verses 4-5, 10-11).

● Although he will die, he will afterwards see results and live long (verse 10-12).

So who is it? Christians and Muslims[57] both claim that Jesus was the Jewish Messiah.

---

[57] See e.g. Matthew 16:16-17 and Sûrah iii.45

Now much becomes clear. In the words of the Bible, the sacrifice of animals was:

> an annual reminder of sins, because it is impossible for the blood of bulls and goats to take away sins... we have been made holy through the sacrifice of the body of Jesus Christ, once for all.[58]

The prophecy in Eden that evil would 'crush the heel' of the human who himself would crush evil, was fulfilled literally as well as in a spiritual sense as a nail was driven into the heel of Jesus.[59]

Abraham's prophecy that 'God will provide himself the sacrificial lamb' was fulfilled in Jesus in the very area (Moriah) where the prophecy was made.

Jesus was executed according to both Christians[60] and non-Christian Jews[61] on the eve of the Passover. At the very time when he was on the cross, the Passover lambs were being killed in the nearby Temple. The 'picture' and the 'reality' were side by side.

The prophecies of Isaiah were fulfilled in the crucifixion and resurrection of Jesus. How, indeed, could anyone live after being pierced and dying, but through resurrection?

Another amazing thing. Psalm 22 seems to almost perfectly describe a crucifixion. Yet it was written over 900 years BC, its writer David had no such experience, and crucifixion was unknown to his people at that time. Why then did he write about it? This becomes clear when Jesus himself uses on the cross its first words: 'My God, my God, why have you forsaken me?'

---

[58] Hebrews 10:3-10

[59] Genesis 3:15. That crucifixion involved this is shown in Ch 8 below

[60] John 19:31

[61] In the Talmudic *Babylonia Sanhedrin*, 43a; the passage is quoted above in Ch 6

When God (in the words of the Qur'ân) 'gave the psalms to David', he gave Psalm 22 as a prophecy about the Messiah, Jesus, who was David's descendant.

Other interpretations?

'Now hang on a minute!' we hear some readers say! 'If it really all fits together so well, why is it that Jews, Christians and Muslims don't all get together and have one religion?' In a sense we find this as mystifying as anyone else.

The Muslim claim is that Jesus never died.[62] Yet this would wreck the whole pattern of sacrifice and prophecy which had been built up by God through centuries of teaching and prophecy to the Jewish nation about the coming Messiah. And both Jews and Muslims accept that this pattern did come from God.

Could it be that the Old Testament prophetic books, for example of Isaiah, were tampered with? Did some enthusiastic early Christians somehow get at them? This has always seemed very unlikely because the Jews themselves have kept the text of Isaiah, meticulously recopying it throughout the generations.

Then, in 1947, an Arab shepherd discovered the Dead Sea Scrolls in a cave in Israel. Amongst multiple copies of Old Testament books was a near-perfect scroll of Isaiah, reliably dated by scholars as just before the time of Christ. This copy (a thousand years older than the previous oldest copy!) had the same text, with all the same prophecies. So now we know that the books *before and at the time of Jesus*, those which would have been accepted *by Jesus himself*, are no different from later versions. Our present book of Isaiah, with its remarkable prophecies, is the one which the Jews had before and during the lifetime of Jesus. All the prophetic passages like the one quoted

---

[62] Sûrah iv.157-8 etc

above from chapter 53 were there before Jesus was born, and were in the passages which he himself read and accepted in his lifetime. There is no possibility that Christians somehow later tampered with the text to make it apparently predict the death of Jesus as a part of God's plans.

Conclusion

If there is a personal Creator-God, is there some pattern in his dealings with humankind? If he has communicated at all, we must surely look for that communication in one of the great 'one-God' faiths?

So let's first recap on what all the three main 'one-God' faiths accept today:

● All believe that God spoke to the Old Testament Jewish people.

● All agree that a sacrificial system was established by those people.

● All agree that that Jewish people were awaiting a special Messiah.

● All must accept (since we now have actual copies) that apparently 'messianic' passages in books like Isaiah were in the Jewish sacred writings before and during the time of Jesus.

So we have the two central questions:

> ** *Was Jesus the prophesied and expected Messiah?*
> ** *Did he fulfil the messianic role of dying as a 'guilt offering' for sin as prophesied in Isaiah 53?*

If we say 'no' to the first question (as would non-Christian Jews), then what possible kind of fulfilment of Isaiah 53 might have been expected other than that which Jesus did? If we say 'yes' to the first question, but 'no' to the second (as would

Muslims), then what could possibly be the meaning of the messianic prophecies of Isaiah?

The whole pattern of sacrifice and growing prophecy of a coming Messiah who would die as a guilt offering for our sin, makes sense only if Jesus really was that Messiah and truly did die (and rise again). If God, as all the three major one-God faiths agree, really did communicate with the Jewish people throughout Old Testament times, it is the Christian view of Jesus which fits into that communication in the most coherent way.

8

Reliable sources?

"Well, Dr Luke, it's not bad for a first attempt, but we think something more racy would sell better."

Myths and history

We've looked at pattern and coherence, but what about evidence and history?

Is there evidence that the historical Jesus is the Jesus of the four Gospels – rather than (say) the one in the Qur'ân or the one in the latest bizarre book on him in the high-street shops? Are the Gospels really 'history'? We believe that the Gospels *are* 'history'. But first we must ask, 'What does this mean?'

The Gospel writer Luke tells us how he set out to compile a reliable account of the important events of Jesus's life, and he went about the task much as any historian would – using proper

sources and eye-witness accounts.[63] Christians may believe his
account is 'inspired' – but this does not imply that Luke wrote it
in some kind of trance or visionary experience. By contrast
Mohammed (for example) wrote his accounts of Jesus 600
years later from visionary experience. The Gospel writers
compiled their accounts from first-century materials –
as history.

No good historian makes up bits to fit his or her theories, but
all historians *select* their material in order to bring out a
particular *perspective.* Any modern book about history
recognises this.[64] Thus, when John's Gospel is open about the
perspective and purpose for which its material was selected,[65] it
is nonetheless 'history'. The writer didn't make it up.

The four Gospels are historical compilations. They are *not*
independently written-down memoirs of four eye-witnesses.
Thus in Matthew, Mark and Luke, there are bits which are
common (word-perfect) to all three, and each pair of them share
bits which are not in the third one. It is clear that all three
Gospels included in their accounts material selected from some
source in common circulation. This material may have been
written (scholars have nicknamed it 'Q') or oral.[66] Historical
writers in those days were not expected to use quotation marks,
so they didn't indicate they were quoting other original
source material.

On another aspect of the 'literary conventions' of the Gospel
writers, it is no problem that some of the events in them
are given in different orders. The writers were concerned with
the reality of the events, not the order. Early Christians
recognised this. One of the earliest Christian writers says that

---

[63] Luke 1:1-4

[64] See, e.g., John Tosh, *Pursuit of History* (1991)

[65] John 20:30-31

[66] See John Wenham, *Redating Matthew, Mark and Luke* (1991)

Mark, 'the interpreter of Peter, wrote down accurately, though not in order, whatever he remembered of the things said or done by Christ.'[67]

Who wrote them?

People often naturally ask, 'Who wrote the Gospels?' The Gospels are, as we noted, compilations rather than modern-type single-author biographies. So then, do we know who compiled them? Some readers may be surprised to find that actually none carry the names of editors or authors as would modern compilations or biographies!

'Luke' claims to be the work of a single compiler (Luke 1:1-4) reasonably identified as the man who also wrote Acts and was Paul's friend Luke.[68]

'Matthew' and 'Mark' carry no claims to be works of individuals and may be best regarded as compilations edited within particular church traditions – although personally (see below in Chapter 10) we do accept as probable the traditional views connecting them in some way respectively with Matthew and with Mark as dependent on Peter.

'John' claims to be compiled within a church tradition dependent on 'the beloved disciple' (John 21:21-24). Scholars don't all agree on who that 'beloved disciple' was, although we personally would accept the traditional and most common identification of him as John, the brother of James, and one of the twelve.

Though, then, we personally accept as probable the 'traditional' associations of the Gospels, they are not essential. The real questions are about the accuracy of the Gospels and the

---

[67] Eusebius, *Ecclesiastical History* iii 39

[68] See e.g. I Howard Marshall, *Luke – Historian and Theologian* (3rd edn. 1988)

early sources they used – not about authorship as such. So how early and authentic are the original Gospels? Where do our familiar four Gospels come from?

Myths and misses

The King James (or Authorised) version of the Gospels (1611) was based on a Greek text reconstructed to the one standardised in the fifth century.[69] By the mid-nineteenth century, translators of the Gospels could also use the ancient Greek copies called the *Codex Vaticanus* and the *Codex Sinaiticus* (found 1844). These two, though then the oldest, still dated from the fourth century, and archaeology had not yet examined evidence for the accuracy of their contents. It was therefore just about plausible at that time to suggest that the Gospels were late and inaccurate compilations.

This has changed. Firstly, earlier copies written on papyrus have been found of parts of gospels. These include the third-century Chester Beatty papyri P45 and P46 (found 1931), the late second-century Bodmer papyri P66 and P75 (found 1956), and the early second-century P52 fragment of John (found 1935). One of the present authors recently saw with his own eyes this early second-century piece, in the Rylands Museum in Manchester. Myths persist, and shortly afterwards he was assured by a Jewish academic that the Gospels were written around the *end* of the second century!

Secondly, archaeology has now been able to assess the Gospels' accuracy on details of life in those times. Luke, for example, gets no less than fifteen Roman governor titles right (praetor, asiarch, tetrarch, lictor, proconsul, procurator, first man etc.), and gets right geographical details which he could

---

[69] The 'Received Text' and 'Stephanos' are just different versions of this

not have known at a later date.[70] John's Gospel contains details showing first-hand knowledge of the terrain.[71]

Some findings have been spectacular. In 1932 a critic claimed that nails were probably not used in crucifixions[72] and the story arose that the Gospels had got it wrong. In 1968 archaeologists found a first-century family tomb north of Jerusalem in which one skeleton had both legs fractured and a seven-inch spike driven through both heel bones.[73] The Gospels were right after all: this archaeological find corroborated the details which they give about the nails, the breaking of the legs to hasten death, etc.

Accuracy and dating

The evidence is very strong that the Gospels were all written in the first century, and that the copies we now have are accurate. We deduce this for the following reasons:

● The Gospels' detailed local knowledge would not have been available to writers in later centuries.

● There had to be time, for example, for papyrus copies of John's Gospel to circulate by the early second century to Egypt where the Rylands fragment mentioned above was found.

● The New Testament is quoted so extensively by early Christian writers from the first century onwards, that virtually all of it would be recoverable from these quotations alone.

● By the third century, translations of the New Testament had been made into Latin, Coptic and Syriac.

---

[70] See our *Reason and Faith*, chap. 3 for details, or any of the further reading listed

[71] See J A T Robinson, *The Priority of John* (1985)

[72] J W Hewitt, 'The Use of Nails in the Crucifixion', *Harvard Theological Review*, Vol. 25, 1932, pp. 29-45

[73] See, e.g. Alan Millard, *Discoveries from the Time of Jesus* (1990), p. 132

Sometimes people wonder if, perhaps, our present four Gospels were just 'selected' out of lots of versions of Jesus' life. Obviously other early accounts must surely have been written, but those which are available today (e.g. the Gnostic material found at Nag Hammadi) are late copies of second-century material. They are mostly collections of supposed teachings of Jesus, with no evidence of first-hand knowledge of the background in which the *real* Jesus of history actually lived.[74] Sometimes Muslims suggest that the so called 'Gospel of Barnabas' is more authentic than the four in the Bible. Since there is no earlier copy of this than a sixteenth century manuscript in Italian, and since it contains demonstrable geographical and historical blunders, this is a particularly bewildering claim and cannot be taken seriously.[75] The four Gospels in the Bible are the only ones available today which have real claims to present the historical Jesus.

Scholars don't entirely agree on the dating of the Gospels. To us the evidence seems to point to all of them being written between about AD 45 and AD 75 – though it is possible that the final compilation of Matthew or John may have been a little later. (Details of the evidence for this can be found in the books listed in the 'Digging Deeper' section at the end of this book.) This would mean that the Gospels were first set down within fifteen to forty-five years of Jesus' death – and were based on even earlier oral or written accounts.

What about the Dead Sea scrolls?

The media love 'conspiracy theories' and startling pronouncements, and a lot of bunkum has been written and

---

[74] See, e.g., B Walker, *Gnosticism* (1983); F F Bruce, *The Canon of Scripture* (1988)

[75] See Professor Norman Anderson, *Islam in the Modern World: A Christian Perspective* (1990), pp. 223-34

broadcast about these scrolls. Found in 1947 near the Dead Sea, they give a picture of the life of a religious community based there between about 170 BC and AD 70. Gospel critics have claimed that the scrolls throw doubt on the Gospels either because the ideas in them are very *similar to* those in the Gospels and so Jesus was not unique, or because the ideas in them are very *different from* the Gospels so Jesus couldn't have been a real first-century Jew. That about covers every possibility!

In fact, whilst some of the religious language used is (hardly surprisingly!) similar to that in the Gospels, there are (as one might expect) both similarities and important differences.[76] Apart from various flights of scholarly fancy in interpreting vague bits in strange ways, there is nothing in the scrolls to cast any doubt on the essential accuracy of the Gospels.[77]

Other evidence

Surviving works from first- and second-century Greek, Roman or Jewish writers are few – but those which we have refer to Christ and Christians much as we would expect.

The earliest is the Jewish historian Josephus, who wrote *The Antiquities of the Jews* in Greek around AD 93. The present Greek versions of his work contain a passage, which may have been edited, but probably originally read something like this:

> At this time there was a wise man called Jesus, and his conduct was good, and he was known to be virtuous. And many people from

---

[76] Archaeologist Professor Alan Millard well summarises these in *Discoveries From the Time of Jesus*, pp. 99-116

[77] This was kindly confirmed to us by the Professor of Hebrew at Oxford, Hugh Williamson – with an explicitness unusual in academic circles!

among the Jews and the other nations became his disciples. Pilate ordered him to be crucified and to die. And those who had become his disciples did not abandon their discipleship. They reported that he had appeared to them three days after his crucifixion and that he was alive. Accordingly, he was thought to be the Messiah about whom the prophets have recounted wonders.[78]

Pliny the Younger was a Roman governor who wrote to the Emperor Trajan around AD 110-3. He wrote of the Christians that they met on a certain day very early, 'when they sang in alternate verses a hymn to Christ as to a god' and bound themselves to a high moral conduct.[79]

The Roman historian Tacitus, writing shortly after, described how Nero tried to shift the blame for the great fire in Rome onto a group of people 'known as Christians'. He adds: 'They got their name from Christ, who was executed by sentence of the procurator Pontius Pilate in the reign of Tiberius.'[80]

This ploy of Nero was also mentioned by Suetonius, writing around AD 120. Suetonius elsewhere mentions that around AD 49 (as we would reckon it) the Emperor Claudius 'expelled the Jews from Rome on account of the riots in which they were constantly engaging at the instigation of Chrestus'.[81] There were often Jewish riots when Jesus was preached (Acts 14:1-6), and a later pagan historian could easily think that 'Chrestus' himself had been present. This seems likely, since 'Christ' is a title, not a name, and it is a title not many Jews would claim. Luke (Acts 18:2) also refers to this act of Claudius.

In Chapter 6 above we mentioned the Jewish traditions,

---

[78] This is the text of an Arabic version found in 1971. For reasons for taking this as near the original, see *Reason and Faith,* pp. 65-6
[79] Pliny, *Epistles* x. 96-7
[80] Tacitus, *Annals* xv, p.44
[81] Suetonius, *Life of Claudius* xv

handed down and embodied in the written Talmud which includes the Mishnah (compiled AD 100-200) and the later Gemera commentaries on the Talmud/Mishnah. They are legal rather than historical, but we quoted the passage which reads:

> Jesus was hanged on the Passover Eve. Forty days previously the herald had cried, 'He is being led out for stoning, because he practised sorcery and led Israel astray and enticed them into apostasy. Whoever has anything to say in his defence, let him come and declare it.' As nothing was brought forward in his defence he was hanged on Passover Eve.[82]

This clearly rejects the Christian interpretation of the events, but nevertheless corroborates the basic historical detail. It recognises that although as a Jew he might have been expected to be stoned to death, he was actually 'hanged' on Passover Eve – as John 19:14 states. Acts 5:30 and 10:39 show that 'hanged' was a natural Jewish way to refer to crucifixion. The sorcery charge presumably relates to his miracles and was made in his lifetime.[83] Elsewhere, other passing references are made to his followers performing miracles.[84]

So the non-Christian sources refer to Jesus and Christians exactly as we would expect. They confirm that Jesus lived in Judaea (Tacitus, Josephus and the Jewish Talmud); that he kept and taught high moral standards (Pliny and Josephus), and that miracles were ascribed to him and his followers (the Talmud), who saw him as a Messiah and divine figure (Pliny and Josephus). He was put to death under Pilate (Tacitus and Josephus) by crucifixion (Josephus and the Talmud). By AD 64

---

[82] *Babylonian Sanhedrin* 43a

[83] Matthew 9:34; Mark 3:22

[84] See F F Bruce, *Jesus and Christian Origins Outside the New Testament* (1974), chap. 4

Jesus' followers were numerous enough in Rome to be blamed by Nero for a great fire, for which they were persecuted (Suetonius and Tacitus).

Conclusion

The Gospels themselves are early and authentic, the text of the copies we now have is accurate, and the most important details of Jesus' life, death and claimed resurrection are reflected in early non-Christian sources. The evidence is that the 'historical' Jesus was essentially the one described in the four Gospels.

9

Dead men tell no tales

"He is not here, he's become a plotting legendary Essene family man growing mushrooms."

'What a nutter!'

'You're out of your mind, Paul – your great learning has finally made you flip!' That was the reaction of the Roman governor Festus when St Paul spoke of the resurrection of Jesus.[85]

A resurrection! Not a temporary restarting of bodily functions, but a new kind of quality of eternal life.

Does it make sense? This, actually, is the question we need to

---

[85] Acts 24:26. In Acts 17:32 some philosophical Athenians reacted somewhat similarly

ask *before* we look at specific evidence for the resurrection of Jesus. Unless an event 'makes sense', no amount of evidence will convince anyone. We've probably all 'seen' women sawn in half (why is it always women?) – but to believe it to have 'really' happened would make no sense, so we assume it was a trick.

The death and resurrection of Jesus 'makes sense' because it is a part of a whole plan of a personal Creator-God to deal with the problem of human sin and to offer us eternal spiritual life. This, in itself, does not prove it is 'true', but it means that we need to take seriously the historical evidence for it.

Evidence

So what is the evidence? Basically it is this:

● A group of Jesus' close friends and followers, dispirited after his execution, claimed to have seen him and spoken to him over a period of about six weeks after his death.

● These were otherwise apparently honest and normal people, of all kinds of characters and backgrounds.

● They were prepared to die for their claims and many did.

● Their beliefs were reflected in early church teaching, and in the Gospel accounts compiled around fifteen to fifty years after Jesus' death.

Let's consider some alternative explanations to actual resurrection.

Alternative 1: a hidden meaning

The extreme versions of this suggest that 'really' the Gospel accounts are in a secret code. Bookshops more interested in controversy (= profit) than truth, carry books by eccentrics who adapt respectable scholarly words like *pesher* or *midrash* (to the astonishment of scholars of all beliefs who know what the words really mean) to imply secret codes only they can crack.[86] Jesus was 'really' married once or twice, had children, and lived to a ripe old age (and, one might almost add without much more fantasy, was occasionally seen sipping lager in Texas – or was that Elvis?). In such flights of unreality the resurrection accounts might mean anything.

To be taken rather more seriously are those who suggest that 'really' the earliest Christians believed in a 'spiritual' resurrection. 'The missing body story,' they say, 'was added later on. Perhaps the people then were too dim to understand a spiritual resurrection, so the writers made it easy for them!'

There are three big problems with this:

1. The writer of John's Gospel uses quite complex language – one would have thought that he, or Luke the educated Greek, could manage to explain a 'spiritual' resurrection. In fact, Luke explicitly emphasises that Jesus' resurrected body had physical properties (Luke 24:37-43).

2. The gospel accounts give a lot of detail – an empty tomb, Jesus appearing first to women etc. If it were only a 'spiritual' thing then one might expect just a kind of camp-fire scene, where they were suddenly all struck with Jesus' memory.

3. The Apostle Paul, in 1 Corinthians 15, refers not to spiritual experience but to historical evidence of the resurrection appearances. Though he does not explicitly mention the empty tomb, he surely intended a 'literal' resurrection – why else would he have been thought mad or stupid by Festus and the Athenians as mentioned earlier in this Chapter?

The accounts seem to refer to a supposed literal event – we have to look for some explanation other than 'spiritualising'.

---

[86] Barbara Thiering, *Jesus the Man* (1992); John Shelby Spong, *Resurrection, Myth or Reality?* (1994)

Alternative 2: a mistake

The accounts record Jesus being taken hurriedly after his death to a nearby family tomb.[87]   Could it just be that Mary Magdalene and the others went to the wrong tomb early on the first Easter Sunday, and the story got out of hand before anyone could correct it?

The problem with this theory is that the tomb belonged to a man of some importance in the community: Joseph of Arimathea. Also present at the entombment was a Jewish council member: Nicodemus. Such men of standing and integrity would surely have denied any untrue rumours and simply produced the body? The authorities, moreover, would surely have known the location of the Jerusalem family tomb of a council member, and would have produced both tomb and body to scotch the rumours.

The same objections apply to the suggestion in a more recent book widely on sale in high-street bookshops. This suggests that people mistook Jesus' brother James, for a resurrected Jesus.[88]   Well, not only is there evidence that some of the disciples were relatives of Jesus and James, but James himself became an early church leader. Did even he make the same mistake? The whole idea seems breathtakingly unlikely!

Finally, could it just have been that grave-robbers stole the body, and so, although at the right tomb, Jesus' followers reached the wrong conclusions? The problem with this is that there was not much of a market for corpses in first-century Jerusalem. Any commercially orientated grave-robber who braved an armed guard to steal a body and leave the grave-clothes behind would have to be very seriously deranged. In any case, it would not explain the actual resurrection appearances to Jesus' disciples.

---

[87] Matthew 27:57-61; Mark 15:42-47; Luke 23:50-55; John 19:38-42
[88] A. N. Wilson, *Jesus* (1992), p. 243

Alternative 3: a fraud

There are various fraud suggestions. The simplest is just that Jesus' disciples stole his body – perhaps as a kind of afterthought. This was actually the earliest counter-theory put about by the authorities.[89] It was still apparently a view accepted by non-Christian Jews when the Christian philosopher Justin Martyr had a debate around the mid-second century.[90] We might call this the 'opportunist' theory.

There are other more elaborate 'fraud theories'. These involve a supposed prior plot between Jesus and a small central group of followers (perhaps including Joseph of Arimathea and Nicodemus) to 'fake' his death and then resuscitate him afterwards.[91] We might call these the 'plot' theories. If, as most of them assume, Jesus actually died by mistake, then there has to be also an element of 'opportunist' cover up – i.e. the body was stolen to start the resurrection legend.

There are three very obvious problems with any of these theories:

1. Jesus and his followers taught a very high moral code – would fraud and deception really be at the centre of their message?

2. The claims to have seen Jesus which were made by significant numbers of people mean that (unless they were exceptionally easily fooled) a large number must have been involved in the cover up if not in the plot.

3. If it were a fake, how can we explain the boldness of the small group of demoralised disciples so soon after Jesus' death? How can we explain their readiness to die?

The versions which have Jesus himself involved in a

---

[89] Matthew 28:13

[90] Justin Martyr, *Dialogue with Trypho*, chap. cviii.

[91] One such is the classic by Hugh Schonfield, *The Passover Plot*, (1965)

supposed 'plot' have even more problems. Would it really be sensible – even if one plotted (say) to be drugged on the cross to look as though dead – to expect to survive a Roman flogging and crucifixion? What would be the point of faking a 'resurrection' if he could simply be recaptured and then be really killed? If Jesus made the kind of claims he made about himself, he either believed them (in which case he would not feel a need to fake a resurrection) or not (in which case he was a charlatan and/or a madman). Would a charlatan really be prepared to go to such risks and lengths for a dubious advantage (after all, he already had lots of followers)? On the other hand, do his words read like those of a madman? They hardly seem so, even to many who are not Christians. But if he was not bad, and not mad, what is there left of this suggestion?

Alternative 4: a hallucination

Did all those who saw Jesus simply hallucinate? Again, there are three main problems:

1. There were apparently lots of different types of people involved, with very different characters, and at different times of day.

2. They actually did not seem to expect a resurrection to happen. The women went to the tomb to anoint the body – not to see if Jesus had risen.[92] The first accounts of the women were received with disbelief.[93]

3. Why didn't the authorities produce the body? Why invent the story that it was stolen?

Hallucination is not very plausible.

---

[92] Mark 16:1; Luke 24:1
[93] Luke 24:11

Alternative 5: a legend

Legends often spring up about remarkable individuals: Ulysses supposedly killed a Cyclops, St George killed a dragon, and King Arthur pulled a sword out of a stone block. If the Gospels were written down long after Jesus' death, couldn't they be full of legends? There are four main problems here:

1. The Gospels were not actually written all that long after Jesus' death – the first perhaps as soon as fifteen years after.

2. All the very earliest references, including early Christian writings from the late first- and early second-century, refer to Jesus's death and resurrection.[94]

3. The actual accounts seem to contain a lot of detail and incidental corroboration.[95]

4. Anyone making up a legend would surely have invented an 'eyewitness' version of Jesus emerging triumphantly from the tomb, or a dramatic first meeting with Peter. The Gospels record neither.

Conclusion

No one can 'prove' that Jesus rose again – at least, not to the satisfaction of anyone who begins by assuming that anything 'supernatural' is impossible and inconceivable. What we *can* do is to show that:

● The accounts of the resurrection date from soon after Jesus' death.

● They were written by honest people preaching a high moral code who were prepared to die for their beliefs.

● The various 'alternative' explanations are not plausible.

---

[94] E.g. 1 Clement xxiv (*c.* AD 96); Ignatius to Ephesus xx (*c.* AD 110); also Polycarp and Justin Martyr in the mid second-century
[95] See the next Chapter

10

Detective work and the resurrection

"So, your grace, what you claim is that while they were asleep your soldiers saw his friends steal the body?"

Elementary, my dear Wotsisname

Any detective knows that six honest and genuine eyewitness accounts of any lengthy event will all differ. People can be in different places and so see different bits of an overall pattern. Different people may notice and record different details, or skip for dramatic effect over boring or irrelevant bits.

Do the four Gospel resurrection passages read essentially like accounts based ultimately on different eyewitnesses? Or are those sceptics and 'theologians' right who argue that the accounts are hopelessly contradictory? The maverick Bishop of

Newark, John Shelby Spong, sees the New Testament as written in a secret code (Midrash) which apparently he alone can crack. He has his own version of 'faith' which describes as legend the basic historical points of the creed he is supposed to avow. He casually remarks: 'The resurrection narratives of the Gospels agree on little if one looks for literal facts...'[96] True or false?

Let's put it another way. Suppose that we begin from the following hypotheses:

1. The four Gospels, although they have some other bits in common, contain four accounts of the resurrection which differ because they draw on different main sources.

2. Each gospel was an anonymous compilation edited in a different church tradition, but there is truth in the early church view that:

● Matthew reflects some input from the disciple Matthew.[97]
● Mark reflects some of Peter's preaching and viewpoint.[98]
● Luke contains a more general compounded account.
● John reflects input from the disciple John Zebedee.[99]

3. Each account reflects the geographical viewpoint and the particular emphasis and selection of its particular source input.

Can the four accounts, then, be fitted into a coherent whole?

Reconstruction

No one can reconstruct such past events with certainty. What we can do is to show that there is at least one reconstruction which enables all the four Gospel accounts to fit together

---

[96] John Shelby Spong, *Resurrection, Myth or Reality?* (1994), p. 235

[97] See e.g. R. T. France, *Matthew* (1985), pp. 30-4 for some support for this

[98] See early church figures Irenaeus (*Adv. Haer* 3.1.2) and Eusebius quoting Papias (*HE* 3.39.14 ff)

[99] See e.g. John A. T. Robinson, *The Priority of John* (1985), for comment

without contradiction (and indeed with some incidental corroboration). This, then, is an outline of what might have happened. Although not strictly necessary for the reconstruction, we also assume in it various family relationships between characters involved, for which we believe there to be good, though not conclusive, evidence.[100]

After Jesus' arrest in Gethsemane, most of the disciples (apart from Peter and John) fled away from Jerusalem, going to Bethany which is about a mile and a half the other way. There they stayed during Jesus' trials and crucifixion.

After the crucifixion, John seems to have taken Jesus' mother Mary straight back to a home he owned or rented in Jerusalem (John 19:27). Peter, after his well-known three denials of Jesus, also went back to John's home – where he is found in John 20:3. Other women who watched the burial (Luke 23:55) also probably went back to John's home. These included Salome (the sister of Jesus' mother, also probably the mother of James and John) and the 'other Mary' who was married to Cleopas (or Clopas – probably Jesus' uncle). Mary Magdalene would also naturally have stayed with them, but Joanna (as wife of Herod's steward Chuza) went to the nearby palace.

Mary the wife of Cleopas and Salome both had sons amongst the disciples at Bethany, and Mary Magdalene[101] may also have had relatives there, so they would have wanted to exchange news. Thus around sunset the next day (so that the trip could be done without breaking the Sabbath) these two Marys (maybe

---

[100] This evidence, and in general more detailed accounts are in John Wenham's *The Easter Enigma* (2nd edn. 1993), and our own *Reason and Faith*

[101] Wenham's book and *Reason and Faith* present the evidence that Mary Magdalene was actually also Mary of Bethany the sister of Lazarus and Martha – though again this helps but is not strictly necessary for our reconstruction.

with Cleopas) walked to Bethany. They stayed there overnight.

Early next morning, Matthew 28:1 (reflecting Matthew who was at Bethany) records how the two Marys set out 'towards dawn'.

They went back to John's house in Jerusalem, where they were joined by Salome and (according to Mark 16:1 which reflects Peter's view) they went on to the tomb 'as the sun was risen'. Luke, with his more global picture, implies that they were joined *en route* by Joanna who, as already noted, would have been staying at the nearby palace.

Meanwhile, Matthew implies, the guards at the tomb understandably fainted at the sight of a shining angel, who rolled back the stone. They then recovered and ran off before the group of women arrived. *No one* saw the actual resurrection.

When the women did arrive at the edge of the garden, Mark makes it clear that they were some way off when they saw that the stone, 'which was very large', (Mark 16:4) had been rolled back. What did they conclude? John 20:2-3 tells us that Mary Magdalene concluded that the body had been taken, and *at that point* she ran back.

Budding Sherlock Holmeses should note two things about this. Firstly, the complex way things fit together. It is *John* who tells us that *just from seeing the stone* Mary Magdalene jumped to her conclusion, and it is *Mark* who tells us that they saw it some way off 'because it was very large'. Together this explains why Mary Magdalene did not see the angels at this point. By this time (as Mark and Luke say) the angels were inside the tomb, and Mary jumped to her conclusion and ran back before actually reaching the tomb or looking inside it.

Secondly, note that John (unlike the other Gospel writers) has mentioned only Mary Magdalene. But note what she says after running back to his house: 'They have taken the Lord out of the tomb and *we* do not know where they have laid him.'(John 20:2). This contrasts with verse 13, where she has by then lost contact with the other women and so says, '*I* do not know where they have laid him.' Verse 2 recorded the plural 'we' because that is actually what she said – and it was seared on John's memory. But it really 'makes sense' only in the light of the other accounts. This is just what we might expect if they are both partial but true accounts reflecting genuine events.

Now two things happened at once. The other women went on (so say Matthew, Mark and Luke) to have a conversation with two angels who were by now inside the tomb. Angels, of course, have wings only in Christmas cards and stained-glass windows – in the Bible they simply look like men. Luke refers to them as 'men' (24:4), but later as 'a vision of angels' (24:13). There is no contradiction. Likewise, Matthew and Mark mention only one angel, whilst Luke mentions two. Perhaps only one spoke, and Matthew and Mark don't think it necessary to mention his companion.

Meanwhile, Mary Magdalene delivered her message to Peter and John, who rushed off to the tomb and found it empty. The other women returned to John's house, where they waited for Peter and John to get back, and then told their story about the angels. Amongst the hearers were Cleopas and his friend, who set off to Emmaus – as recorded by Luke. Their conversation on the road (Luke 24:13-33) shows that they knew exactly what the women, Peter and John, would have told them. Magadelene followed Peter and John back to the tomb – missing them on the way – and met Jesus at the tomb on her own (John 20:11-18).

The women had been given by the angels a message for 'the disciples'. Having given the message to Peter and John back at John's house, they were running towards Bethany to tell the rest of the disciples when Jesus himself met them (Matthew 28:9). Matthew's Gospel records the meeting with Jesus immediately after the meeting with the angels – just as Matthew himself heard it recounted at Bethany.

Where, then, are all the supposed contradictions? If the

accounts fitted together more easily or if they all included exactly the same details, then we might suspect collusion. As it is, they do indeed look like accounts with input from different eyewitness sources. They certainly do not look like legend or fantasy. Either a first-century Agatha Christie has cleverly constructed the four separate accounts, or else they are independently compiled records of genuine events.

11

I think, therefore I am – I think...

"René! Have you done them dishes yet,
or are you still thinking?"

Calling all humans!

We can't imagine what it must be like to be (say) a dolphin or a gorilla, but we do find the experience of being human pretty amazing!

As humans, we are not only aware of sensations, but can be reflective about them. We also use language in a special way, in a structure which relates concepts and includes abstract ideas. We 'think' both in imagination and in words and sentences. We *consciously* make decisions, i.e. we are *aware* of doing so. All of this is implied when each of us uses the word 'I'.

Now let's get into some heavy thinking about reality. Most of what we 'know' is somehow deduced or inferred from sensations. But the most certain thing that I 'know' is that there is an 'I' experiencing the sensations. René Descartes' words, 'I think therefore I am' may not be strict 'logic', but they make sense to most of us – and you don't have to be a philosopher to understand what he meant.

I may be mistaken about whether what I am experiencing is 'real' (whatever that means). A particular 'experience', for example, might be a dream, or the result of eating magic mushrooms, or a giant hologram, or something physical. But what I cannot doubt is that there is a 'me' having the experience.

A 'mind' is another way of describing this essential 'me' – and the relationship between 'me' (mind) and the physical world (matter) has been long discussed by philosophers. What are the main suggestions they have come up with?

Nothing buttery

We often try to understand a thing by studying how each separate part of it works. Science often does the same. The process of 'reducing' something to its parts is a proper element of scientific method.[102] Medical science has progressed when parts of the body have been looked at separately as mechanical systems, then studied at the chemical level. Chemical reactions may sometimes be better understood by studying the underlying atomic movements.

The real problem comes, though, when this kind of 'reduction' is seen not just as a tool, but as implying that a whole is no more than the sum of its parts. The phrase 'nothing but' is then often used, and the apt term 'nothing buttery' to describe this has been popularised by Professor D. M. MacKay. The major

---

[102] This is sometimes called 'methodological reductionism', see, e.g.
Arthur Peacocke, *Reductionism in Academic Disciplines* (1985)

problem with it is that entirely new properties can 'emerge' when parts are fitted together. A sonata is more than a collection of musical notes, and exploring the effects of a sonata by looking at the individual notes misses the point – although one early 'reductionist' philosopher suggested doing exactly this![103]

Even in biology there seems to be an increasing awareness of 'holism' – the need to look at a system as a whole. In 1974 a leading biologist wrote:

> ...a majority of biological concepts, such as cell, organ, Mendelian population, species, genetic homoeostasis, predator, trophic level, etc., cannot be defined in physiochemical terms.[104]

If anything, holistic awareness has increased since then. It is not that higher-order physical systems do not obey the lower-order physical laws – it is just that new properties emerge which cannot be 'reduced'. Even Richard Dawkins, an avowed 'hierarchical reductionist', denies the cruder form of the whole as 'nothing but the sum of the parts'![105]

If it is, in fact, questionable how far the reductionist approach works for, say, explaining biology in terms of chemistry. In the area of 'mind' it is even less convincing.

It's those philosophers who want to convince us, effectively, that we don't really exist (i.e. that mind is an illusion or an accidental by-product of 'real' material reactions) who usually use some form of 'nothing buttery'. David Hume, the eighteenth-century founder of British 'empiricism' (a philosophy which sees experience as the only source of

---

[103] Marcus Aurelius, *Meditations* bk. 11

[104] F J Ayala, *Studies in the Philosophy of Biology: Reduction and Related Problems* (ed F J Ayala and T Dobzhansky, 1974), Introduction

[105] Richard Dawkins, *The Blind Watchmaker* (1986) p. 13

knowledge), was definitely a star 'nothing butterer' amongst philosophers. He wrote:

> What we call a mind is nothing but a heap or collection of different perceptions, united together by certain relations, and supposed, though falsely, to be endowed by a perfect simplicity and identity.[106]

How bizarre. According to him, only experiences are real – but there is no one there to experience them! No wonder he later admitted that this part of his scheme wasn't very convincing!

But the more common and less subtle version of this is to say that humans are 'nothing but atoms and molecules'. On this view, mind, personhood, love, beauty, justice, etc. are all reducible to the physical. A number of well-known writers certainly sound as though this is exactly what they are saying – even though their small print contains a lot of 'toning down'. T Nagel argued for a 'physicalism' which held that

> a person, with all his psychological attributes, is nothing over and above his body, with all its physical attributes.[107]

Figures like E O Wilson, Richard Dawkins and Peter Atkins seem to assume that the only 'valid' kind of explanation is a scientific one and that ultimately everything will be reducible to nothing but such terms. Even though the idea of a scientific 'theory of everything' has a seemingly insurmountable problem of logic (based on Godel's theorem[108]), they talk as though it

---

[106] David Hume, *A Treatise of Human Nature* (1739), bk. 1, chap. iv, p. 2. The 'Logical Positivists' of the 1930s-50s followed this

[107] T Nagel, 'Physicalism', *Phil Review* 74 (1965), pp. 339-56

[108] Godel's theorem is too technical to explain here, but see, e.g., Rodney D Holder, *Nothing But Atoms and Molecules?* (1993), pp. 223-5

were a possible goal. In taking this approach they ignore the objections of fellow scientists (like Einstein, as quoted earlier), philosophers and logicians.

The 'I' fights back

The attempts to explain away 'mind' remain unconvincing, and it is not just Christians who find them so. The philosopher John Searle, in his Reith lectures, wrote:

> I'm conscious I AM conscious. We could discover all kinds of startling things about ourselves and our behaviour; but we cannot discover that we do not have minds, that they do not contain conscious, subjective, intentionalistic mental states; nor could we discover that we do not at least try to engage in voluntary, free, intentional actions.[109]

In a recent book, the Professor of Philosophy at Warwick University writes:

> Consciousness, and the further ability to be self-conscious and reflect about one's own states, are eliminated by a scientific programme at the cost of bringing into question the very status of science.[110]

How could scientific knowledge be possible if there is no 'knower' there to know it?

Ironically, in twentieth-century subatomic physics the 'observer' is actually more than an incidental to what happens to the particles. There is a sense in which the act of observing determines which of a set of potential universes we turn out to

---

[109] John Searle, *Minds Brains and Science* (1984)
[110] Roger Trigg, *Rationality and Science* (1993)

be in.[111] Far from abolishing 'mind', modern physics reasserts the centrality of the observer.

So if both mind and matter are 'real', what *sensible* theories are there to explain their relationship?

Two are most common. The first (sometimes called 'perspectivalism') stresses that there can be levels of meaning for the same event. The professor and brain expert D M MacKay has illustrated this with an EXIT sign. To analyse it in terms of its chemical constituents would be to miss the point – at a different level entirely it carries a *message*. Likewise, he says, there is an 'I-story' (an inside view of events) and an 'O-story' (an observer's view of events). Seen thus a human is:

> a unity with many complementary aspects, each needing to be reckoned with at a different logical level, and all interdependent.[112]

In this view 'mind' and 'brain' do not interact, but are aspects of the same thing – each real at a different level. There are both Christians and non-Christians who accept a view similar to this.

We personally find the idea of 'levels' useful, but we also believe that there is a sense in which mind and brain do interact. This idea goes back to René Descartes (the 'I think, therefore I am' man), but has been strongly argued in recent years by amongst others the Christian medical brain expert Sir John Eccles and the non-Christian philosopher Sir Karl Popper.[113] Eccles is a respected scientist, and Popper has been 'widely described as the most important philosopher of the 20th century'.[114] The 'mind' is not, of course, pictured as being in the

---

[111] This is explained, e.g., by Stephen Hawking in *Black Holes and Baby Universes* (1993), pp. 38-9

[112] D M Mackay, *Brains, Machines and Persons* (1980), p. 80

[113] e.g. in *The Self and Its Brain* (1977)

[114] *The Independent on Sunday* (18.9.94), p. 3. Paul Marston first studied the philosophy of science under Popper at the London School of Economics in 1967

body like some kind of 'dalek' sitting in an external machine. Mind and body are one – and if you kick my leg it is 'me' who feels it. Nevertheless, it is right to speak of mind and brain *interacting* (sometimes this view is poshly termed 'Dualistic Interactionism'!).

Popper and Eccles also write of our common experience of exercising acts of the will – the almost indelible impression we have of some kind of 'free will'. Could a 'super-scientist' in theory predict absolutely everything we would do – and would this show that our feeling of free will was an illusion?

Interestingly, since 1928 the scientific 'uncertainty principle' has accepted that at the very lowest subatomic level events can be predicted only in terms of probability. This is (rather mind-bogglingly, to most of us) not just because we don't have accurate enough instruments, for the results of such events are not even predictable *in principle*. Their future would remain unpredictable (according to physics) even if we had perfect information about their present state. There is no strict determinism at the subatomic level, and larger-scale events are generally predictable only because of the 'law of averages'.

So are our brains deterministic and are human decisions therefore in principle totally predictable? If it turns out that some decisions are 'tipped' one way or the other by a very few atomic particles, then they may not be. This kind of suggestion was made from the very start of the uncertainty principle by the leading physicist Eddington, who suggested that 'mental decision' might determine atomic behaviour.[115] Amongst more recent sub-atomic physicists, the Oxford Professor Roger Penrose has shown a continued interest in connections between mind and atomic uncertainty.[116]

Some human decisions may be predictable because the

---

[115] Arthur Eddington, *The Nature of the Physical World*, p. 332
[116] See, e.g., Roger Penrose, *Shadows of the Mind...* (1994)

person is known to have already made up their mind, and many can be predicted with high degrees of probability. But present atomic physics leaves room for belief that human free will maintains a certain degree of unpredictability in individual human decision.

There is, of course, always a danger of over-simplifying, but it appears from all this that present science says nothing to prevent us accepting what seems our common experience of 'mind'. This is that we have some kind of 'free will' in which our minds 'make decisions' which are carried out by our bodies.

The God bit

Once I accept that there really is an 'I' – a personal being – two obvious questions are raised:

● Did any 'personhood' exist before mankind arrived?
● Does our 'personhood' finish at physical death or does it survive?

Christianity claims to answer both of these questions. To the first the answer is that personhood is not some accidental by-product of matter operating under laws of blind undesign. Rather, personhood, in the being of God, was primary – it is the physical world which is derivative and was created by him. We are personal, moral beings with free will – made in the image of a personal, moral God who has free will. This was how the early Christians understood Genesis 1-3.[117] No one should deny that there are profound mysteries remaining in this, but it is a view which 'makes sense', unlike the view that human personhood and consciousness just 'popped up' by accident.

To the question of the survival of the person after physical

---

[117] See our *Reason and Faith* for much more detail of this

death the Bible also gives an answer. The early chapters of Genesis symbolise great truths in terms of two trees.[118] When God created mankind he offered them a 'tree of life' – an opportunity that spiritual life as distinct from physical life would never end. But he also gave them a moral sense and moral choice symbolised by the 'tree of the knowledge of good and evil'. Then, through human sin, the offer of eternal life was forfeited. This, as we have seen, led on to the unfolding of a plan by God to deal with sin through the death and resurrection of Jesus. In a nutshell: 'For sin pays its wage – death; but God's free gift is eternal life in union with Christ Jesus our Lord.'[119] God makes the offer of eternal life, but for those who steadfastly refuse to accept this offer, the Bible speaks of the 'second death' or being 'punished with everlasting destruction'.[120] We take this to be the destruction of the person in an eternal (i.e. an irrevocable) judgement – analogous to the destruction of the body at physical death.

Conclusion

Personal consciousness and identity is a reality, but also a mystery. We suggest that it points to the existence of a personal Creator, and that Christianity again makes the most sense of it all.

---

[118] We leave open at this point whether the trees were also 'literal' – whether they were or not does not affect the symbolism

[119] Romans 6:23

[120] Revelation 20:14; 2 Thessalonians 1:9

12

It's a miracle!

"You're late home dear, and our daughter is being impossible today!"

What's a miracle?

A newspaper headline 'It's a miracle!' may be followed by an account of any unusual or unexpected event. We suggest, however, that 'miracles' fall into two broad types:

● Type 1: Those which are unusual, perhaps involving remarkable 'coincidence' but which involve no alteration in the 'laws of nature'.
● Type 2: Those events which do involve an alteration in the usual physical sequences found in the 'laws of nature'.

To illustrate this think about the following two stories:

(i) An atheist and a Christian are going across a remote desert in a Landrover when they run out of petrol. Knowing that no one ever passes that way for months on end, the Christian falls to her knees in fervent prayer, whilst the atheist prays more surreptitiously! After ten minutes, over the hill comes a Jeep with an Englishman, a Scotsman and an Irishman in it (no it's not that joke!), and they lend them a can of petrol. 'Praise the Lord, it's a miracle,' says the Christian. 'Just a coincidence,' says the atheist.

(ii) An atheist and a Christian are going across a remote desert in a Landrover when they run out of petrol. Knowing that no one ever passes that way for months on end, the Christian falls to her knees in fervent prayer, whilst the atheist prays more surreptitiously! After ten hours, nothing happens. 'I have the faith!' says the Christian, and pours a large canister of orange juice into the petrol tank. The engine roars into life and they drive to the next water hole. 'It's a miracle!' says the Christian. 'There must be some explanation,' says the atheist.

The first incident is either 'just coincidence' or a type-1 miracle – how it is seen depends on one's view of the world! Neither view is any more 'rational' than the other, though it is amazing how many atheists pray when in danger or distress!

The second incident cannot be 'just coincidence' – we all know it to be *impossible* for a car engine to run on orange juice. This was a type-2 miracle. You might think that, faced with such a situation, the atheist would fall to her knees and admit there was a God. Not necessarily. Back in safety, a number of alternatives would occur to her. Perhaps it had really all been a hallucination. Perhaps the petrol tank had not really been empty. Perhaps the Christian had tried to trick her. The saying 'seeing is believing' is, in reality, not true. No conceivable amount of evidence could convince someone who is unwilling to alter their world-view to admit a type-2 miracle.

Does science rule out type-2 miracles ?

If we think about it, a universe with *no* regularity would be uninhabitable. It is therefore hardly surprising that we find regularity in the universe we are in. The methodical study of that regularity results in what we call 'science'. It involves inventing concepts and laws with which we can understand that regularity and predict future experience.

So can 'science' tell us whether the physical chains of cause and effect are *totally* invariable? No. The success of any scientific law can be decided only by experience and observation – and experience and observation are also the only way to tell whether there are ever exceptions.

Sometimes, of course, a 'scientific' explanation may be found for something which was previously thought to be a type-2 miracle. Thus, e.g., lightning may turn out to be part of the normal physical cause-effect of electrical discharge – rather than Zeus or Thor chucking thunderbolts because of indigestion. But this kind of thing cannot show that type-2 miracles *never* occur. To give an analogy, the discovery that a painting thought to be a Rubens is actually a fake does not prove that there are no paintings by Rubens. We could rule out type-2 miracles altogether only if there were good reason to believe the very idea of a type-2 miracle to be nonsensical.

Do type-2 miracles make sense?

The term 'miracle' itself implies not some kind of

inexplicable uncaused event, but one which is brought about by a different order of causality. This reflects the Christian view of reality, where the physical world is dependent on God for its continuing existence. Christian thinkers have always believed this.[121] Thus it is God who creates the winds[122] – although they are part of natural processes. God is not merely in the 'gaps' in natural causes, he is the reason why natural processes continue to operate.

To illustrate this, we need to use language which contains implicit and explicit analogy. This does not worry us.[123] Even within physical science there is use of 'analogical' language (picture language in a sense) to help understand unimaginable phenomena (e.g. sub-atomic reactions) in terms of everyday experience. We picture electrons as 'particles' and talk of 'spin' – though they are in most respects really not much like spinning billiard balls.

We are, then, similarly in need of pictures to understand the Christian view of God's relationship to the world. One analogy for this might be a television screen.[124] In, say, a cartoon, one can observe 'cause and effect' taking place – but this is different from the 'cause' of the picture being there at all. An even better analogy might be, say, the writer-director of a film. There are 'causes' and 'effects', personal interactions etc., *within* the film, but this is different from the 'cause' of the whole story and film being there at all (i.e. the writer-director).

---

[121] Our *Reason and Faith* (p. 133) cites John Chrysostom, John Calvin, Jean Buridan, Robert Boyle and William Buckland as examples

[122] Amos 4:13

[123] See also Ian Barbour's works e.g. *Myths, Models and Paradigms* (1974)

[124] D M MacKay gave this analogy in *Science and Christian Faith Today* (1963)

God, in this view, had to give us a physical world which had general predictability – otherwise it would have been uninhabitable. In science we study the usual patterns in the physical reality he sustains. But there is no reason to suppose that he cannot sometimes vary these patterns – i.e. produce a type-2 miracle. It is important to realise that these are not 'uncaused' events, but arise due to an interplay of 'forces' outside the purely physical. There is, on this view, a complex interplay of the spiritual 'forces' of God, other spiritual realities, and the minds and spirits of humans involved. We put the word 'forces' in inverted commas because they are not measurable physical forces in the usual sense – but we have no other language with which to speak of them.

Obviously, if there were no reality *but* the physical, then there still might be events which were 'impossible' in terms of normal scientific laws. We could, however, hardly call them 'miracles', since they would lack any purpose or meaning and would simply appear as irrational and inexplicable

Type-2 miracles, then, make sense, but only as part of a world-view which involves dimensions of reality other than the physical.

Are miracles too improbable to consider?

There are those today who basically follow the same kind of approach as the eighteenth century philosopher and 'nothing butterer' David Hume. In his philosophy:[125]

1. Everything is supposed to be decided on the basis of observation and experience.

2. Assessing the truth of any reported event is a balance of probabilities.

---

[125] David Hume, *An Enquiry Concerning Human Understanding* (1748)

3. The *a priori* improbability of anything 'violating the laws of nature' is so great that 'overwhelming human testimony' would be necessary in order to make us accept it.

4. The right kind of human testimony for miracles (reliable, sophisticated, first-hand witnesses of incontrovertible miracles) is lacking.

5. Also, there is a natural human tendency to exaggerate, and miracles are usually more reported among 'ignorant and barbarous nations'.

6. Miracles, therefore, have not happened and do not happen.

Extraordinary! Claiming to begin from accepting that observation and experience must decide whether miracles do in fact occur, he finishes up by denying that they possibly can – however strong the testimony is that they have done! And Christians sometimes get accused of prejudice!

Evidence

The Gospels record Jesus performing what seem to be type-2 miracles, and they have been noted throughout church history.[126] But what about today?

Accounts of what appear to be type-2 miracles have been given in the last couple of decades by countless numbers of apparently sane, normal, intelligent Christians – many with medical training. Numerous cases of miracles happening have been reported by Christian leaders whom we know (e.g. Colin Urquhart, John Wimber, Gerald Coates, Peter Gammons,[127]) and there have also been miracles in our own personal experience.[128]

---

[126] See our *Reason and Faith* p.156, or Rex Gardner, *Healing Miracles: A Doctor Investigates* (1986)

[127] For these see the recommended further reading at the end of this book

[128] *Reason and Faith*, chap. 9

The blind see, the deaf hear, the lame walk, and the dying recover. These are not exceedingly rare occurrences, but happen more often than may be realised.

Funnily enough, in one way science has made the evidence for type-2 miracles stronger, not weaker. In the first century, it might be said, medical diagnosis was very poor, and perhaps the apparent 'healings' were just things which would have got better anyway. Nowadays, however, medical diagnosis can be clearly confirmed – and yet there are still things for which it is almost impossible even to conceive explanations other than that a type-2 miracle has occurred.

Miracles, proof and puzzles

We regard the reality of type-2 miracles as a significant piece of evidence for the truth of Christianity. It is not, of course, a 'proof'. A really determined sceptic can always think up some way around it:

- The diagnosis was mistaken.
- The illness was 'really psychological'.
- The 'recovery' was illusory.
- The whole episode was a trick.

All that we can say is that these explanations, whilst they may be true of some examples, are literally incredible for some of the cases known to us. The reality of miracles, whilst never a watertight 'proof', can certainly be a 'sign' for those open-minded enough to accept that there might be a powerful Creator-God.

This does not mean that there are no puzzles. Why don't *all* the people prayed for recover? If God can 'intervene' in *some* instances, then why doesn't he stop *all* the sin and suffering? There are no quick and complete answers.

We do know that God is not a 'puppet master' who strictly determines everything which happens. The Bible teaches us that there is a warfare afoot between the forces of good and evil – and human prayer is a part of this warfare.[129] God *will* one day stop all the sin and suffering – but this will mean that the Day of Judgement has come, and that is not always what those who call for it have in mind!

We cannot pretend to understand everything. But we do believe that type-2 miracles happened in Jesus' ministry, they happen today, and they help confirm the rationality of belief that Christianity is true.

---

[129] Ephesians 6. See our book *God's Strategy in Human History* (1973, 1989) for further biblical details on this

13

The experience of God

"Excuse me, Miss - may I ask when was the last time you had a transcendental religious experience?"

What kind of experiences?

Let's think about kinds of human religious experience:

1. **A sense of awe:** Sometimes a person will experience a sense of awe or an intuitive recognition that there is something behind the physical universe. We speak here not of logic and deduction, but of a personal experience in looking at nature – whether it be a desert night sky, a scene of mountains and lakes, or the intricacies of life under a microscope. This feeling does not, of course, have to involve belief in a truly personal God – but it is a kind of religious experience.

2. **Inner conviction:** Someone can have the inner conviction that God has been present with him or her in a particular situation. This can vary from a quiet conviction to an overwhelming sense of a divine presence in a situation which may itself vary from the mundane to extreme difficulty.

3. **Charismatic experience:** Sometimes people feel as though God is working or speaking *through* them. The word *'charisma'* means gift, and it is as though God is giving them a gift to use for others. This could involve speaking in a strange tongue, feeling a conviction that a message has been given, feeling 'anointed' in the preaching of a sermon, having a 'knowledge' about someone else which could not naturally have come, or being used in a physical healing.[130]

4. **Visionary experience:** Some have an experience of literally seeing a vision or hearing a voice – like the Apostle Paul when he saw a light and heard the voice of Jesus on the Damascus road or John when he wrote the book of Revelation.[131]

5. **Outward manifestation:** Just as may be found in the Bible, many people today experience sensations in their bodies – falling down,[132] deep sleep,[133] laughing,[134] weeping,[135] trembling,[136] etc. Those experiencing God in this way sometimes look as if they are drunk![137] There was nothing essentially new in the so-called 'Toronto experience' involving some of these things, which came to some British churches in 1994.

---

[130] 1 Corinthians 12:8-11

[131] Acts 10:10; Revelation 1:10; also Acts 10:9-18, etc

[132] Compare Matthew 17:6; Acts 9:4; Revelation 1:17

[133] Compare Daniel 10:9; Genesis 15:12

[134] Compare Psalm 126:2

[135] Compare Ezra 10:1; Nehemiah 8:9

[136] Compare Daniel 10:10; Habakkuk 3:16

[137] 1 Samuel 1:13; Jeremiah 23:9; Acts 2:13; Ephesians 5:8

Some points about these kinds of religious experience. They are not, of course, 'watertight' categories – and some experiences may come under two or more of them. They are also experiences which are claimed both by Christians and non-Christians. So what are we to make of them?

One way Christianity

As Christians, we believe that the Bible (or 'Scripture') is 'inspired', and that the message it contains – read aright – is an assured message from God. We believe this not only from inner conviction, but also because of Jesus' own teaching on the Old Testament and about his purposes for choosing Apostles.[138] But the Bible itself implies that it is not the only way in which God speaks to people. Romans 1:18-2:16 speaks of two streams of humanity: those who repent and put their trust in God and those who are unrepentant and without faith. Even to those without any Bible, God speaks through nature (Romans 1:20) and conscience (2:15) – this is kindness which is meant to lead them into repentance (2:4). He may also sometimes speak in dreams[139] or in visions.[140]

Jesus claimed to be the only way for a person to be right with God.[141] To accept this claim is to accept that anyone who has been right with God – before or after Jesus came – has been so through Jesus. But it does not mean that all of them have heard about Jesus – and obviously, Jesus was not known to faithful Jews in the Old Testament, let alone non-Jews like Melchizedek and Job.

---

[138] See John Wenham, *Christ and the Bible* (1993)
[139] E.g., Daniel 4:4 (and see 4:27); Matthew 2:12
[140] Daniel 5:5; Acts 10:3
[141] John 14:6

This is emphatically *not* saying that 'all religions lead to God'. Such a thing would be foolish – since not all religions say the same thing. What it *is* saying is that we must beware of assuming that the only genuine experiences of God are those of Christians – we must not limit God in this way.

Assessing experience

Those 'reductionists' who (as we noted in Chapter 11) argue that only the physical is real and that consciousness is some kind of illusion, could apply the same approach to spiritual experience, even if it involves some outward manifestation. 'It is,' they proclaim, 'nothing but a brain malfunction, a psychosis, or a survival device of human genes. It's "all psychological".'

Now, obviously there are times when (say) mentally ill people may have visions or experiences which resemble those of saints. But this does not prove that there are no *genuine* religious experiences. A comparison might be that mentally ill people may, at times, hallucinate (for example) snakes – but this does not prove that there are no *real* experiences of snakes. Whether my particular perception of a 'snake' is real, hallucination, or dream, has to be decided by criteria other than the pure experience. The question is whether that experience 'makes sense'.

We suggest, then, that religious experiences cannot be 'written off' as 'all psychological', but that exactly *what* is being experienced needs to be decided according to whether it makes sense.

Archbishop George Carey, discussing this, suggested that we should look at the character of the person having the experience, and the moral effect of it on their life.[142]

---

[142] George Carey, *The Great God Robbery* (1989) p. 97

On these criteria, the claims of many Christians to have had a personal experience of God, Jesus Christ and the Holy Spirit, must surely count for something. Religious experiences – as a part of a general pattern of experience of consciousness and of the miraculous – make sense.

Differences and puzzles

Religious experience – and even more, the way we talk about it to others – is shaped by what we expect and by the language we are taught. This is inevitable, though we perhaps need to beware of over-conformity. Some Christians have had a 'conversion experience', others are repentant and in a relationship with God, but without dating it from some specific time.

We cannot always know why particular individuals have particular experiences. There was, for example, a report in *The Independent* on 11th August 1994 of a young Greek Orthodox woman in Syria who had visions, stigmata and occasional strange physical manifestations of oil on her hands. The report seems to show that these things brought her into a deep spiritual experience and a heightened concern for others. Whilst we would have preferred her to have had more 'Protestant' visions, and whilst we cannot 'explain' why she in particular should have been chosen, we see no reason to deny that her experience of God is genuine (although, of course, to be fully convinced we would need much more information). Jesus warned us against too hasty judgement of those 'not in our set' doing miracles in his name![143] There are, of course, some who pretend to have experiences or to be able to heal in order to get attention or money – but the existence of 'fakes' should not make us

---

[143] Mark 9:39-40

dismiss the real thing. We simply need to be careful in our assessment of claims.

Christians differ in the degree to which they have each of the above five types of religious experience. They also differ in their degree of 'certainty' about themselves, about God and their faith. Those who are the most 'certain' are not always either the most Christ-like or the most productive in their Christian lives! God calls Christians to commitment, trust, obedience and faithfulness – it is this (and not 'feelings' or 'experiences') on which they believe their right relationship with God is grounded.

Having said this, obviously we may bear in mind the old saying: 'He that expecteth nothing shall in no wise be disappointed'! Religious experiences are real and they make sense, but they may have to be sought after.

Conclusion

The personal experience of God has been central to Bible-based Christianity throughout history. Types and degrees of such experience may vary, but it does form a part of human experience, and it does 'make sense' as a part of the evidence that there is a personal Creator-God.

Response

14

Over to you!

"Pete, are you sure you've got this faith thing sussed?"

Logic and relationship

We have seen that nature, history and human/religious experience together point to Christianity as the view of reality which makes the most sense. There is good evidence for its claim to be the truth about God, the universe and ourselves.

But 'God' is not merely the logical conclusion of a series of deductions. He is a *person*. The point of it all is not just to conclude something about him, but to get to know and experience him.

Decision or delay?

Christianity involves a personal commitment. There may, however, be some who, although they accept the evidence for the truth of Christianity, want to delay taking any action. Here are some of the most common reasons for putting it off:

* I'm too young/too old (*delete as necessary).
* I'm not good enough/not bad enough (*delete as necessary).
* I don't know all the answers and still have a lot of questions, such as:

What about Adam and Eve?
How did Jonah swallow the whale (or whatever)?
Why isn't the world a nicer place?
Why are there hypocrites in church?

Jesus makes no exceptions to the need to receive him – old or young, good (and 'nobody's perfect!') or bad. We take seriously the various problems and difficulties in Christian belief,[144] but if we waited until all our problems and questions were solved, then we'd never do anything about anything.

This is true of other relationships. It is good to think a bit, for example, about marriage before entering into it. But if we waited in the hope of one day knowing everything about relationships and about the other person, we would die single.

Commitment to Christ is not 'blind faith', but it does involve a trust that there are answers to questions we may have.

Becoming a Christian

Jesus promised all those who received him and believed on

---

[144] We do so in our other books, *That's A Good Question* (1979), *Reason and Faith* (1989) and hope to write further publications on such issues

his name the power to become the children of God.[145] But how does someone 'receive' Christ? The simple message of the early Christians was: *Repent towards God and believe on the Lord Jesus Christ*, and that's the answer.

Repentance

The first essential in repentance towards God is the readiness to be as honest before him and with ourselves as we are able.[146] The second essential is a willingness to follow his plan and purpose for our lives: his way, lifestyle, or whatever.

These two features are common to all who accept God's offer of a relationship with him, but there are many differences. Some may feel that they hardly believe God is really there; others are convinced in their minds but have never experienced the reality of God in their lives. Many feel very sure that God is there, but feel very hesitant about commitment to obeying him, when it might involve so much. Some see fully how far their own lives fall short of the perfect life lived by Christ, others have little consciousness of the guilt which belongs to the wrongs they know they have done.

We must be willing to accept ourselves *as we are*, for we are seeking to begin an individual relationship with God. We must not try to copy others, or expect exactly the same experience to follow. It is with this honesty of mind that we should tell God that from now on we want to go his way. But this alone does not make someone a Christian.

Faith

A true Christian is one who 'believes in' and 'receives' the Lord Jesus Christ.[147] In the New Testament meaning, 'believe

---

[145] John 1:12
[146] Luke 8:15
[147] Acts 16:31; John 1:12

in' does not just mean 'believe about' but to 'put faith and trust in'. A sick person is not made well by knowledge about a doctor, or even by belief that a doctor can heal, but by the doctor him/herself when the person places themselves in the doctor's hands. Our knowledge about and confidence in the doctor helps us to go to him/her. But the point is that we must place ourselves in the doctor's hands. In the same way we may know much or little about Christ, and our confidence in him may be great or small, but the real point is an act of faith whereby we commit ourselves into his hands. It is those who actually *call* on the Lord who are saved.[148] This 'calling' involves being prepared to turn in repentance, confessing in prayer and asking God for new spiritual life. The confidence which Christians rightly have in their Lord may develop after this act of faith.

The outcome

In the relationship with Christ which has begun, the new Christian should begin to read the Bible seriously, starting, we suggest, with the Gospel of John. The Bible will become a living book as God speaks to him or her through it, and prayer will become a time of real sharing.

Here are two important points to note. For those brought up in Christian homes, relationship with God does not always start at some recognised point in time. They should not feel that they have to 'make up' a date of conversion because some others have one! The real point is to ask themselves whether they are *now* living in repentance, trusting in Jesus, and open to his spirit. God deals with people differently – even if the end object may be similar.

Likewise a word of warning to any who *do* turn to God at a specific time. After the 'dramatic' stories of conversions they

---

[148] Romans 10:13

have heard, some people find their own experiences during conversion less 'dramatic' than they expected. They 'feel no different', and no blinding lights from heaven shine! Experiences do vary, but sometimes they may later find that when they try to talk about their own experience, the only language they can use is what once seemed to them dramatic! Anyway, the vital point is to be real with God – don't worry about 'experience'.

The Gospels record an incident which we have found to be helpful to some people during their conversion and first few weeks of Christian experience:

> Then he (Jesus) made the disciples embark and go on ahead to the other side, while he sent the people away; after doing that, he went up the hill-side to pray alone. It grew late, and he was there by himself. The boat was already some furlongs from the shore, battling with a head-wind and a rough sea. Between three and six in the morning he came to them, walking over the lake. When the disciples saw him walking on the lake they were so shaken that they cried out in terror: 'It is a ghost!' But at once he spoke to them: 'Take heart! It is I; do not be afraid.' Peter called to him: 'Lord, if it is you, tell me to come to you over the water.' 'Come,' said Jesus. Peter stepped down from the boat, and walked over the water towards Jesus. But when he saw the strength of the gale he was seized with fear; and beginning to sink, he cried, 'Save me, Lord.' Jesus at once reached out and caught hold of him, and said, 'Why did you hesitate? How little faith you have!' Then they climbed into the boat; and the wind dropped. And the men in the boat fell at his feet, exclaiming, 'Truly you are the Son of God.'[149]

Was this ghost-like figure, so far removed from Peter's everyday experience, really Jesus? His doubts resolved only after he had stepped out, and he could later say: 'Truly you are the Son of God.'

---

[149] Matthew 14:22-23 (NEB)

He had to act upon what he already knew, and this action was started in talking to the indistinct figure: 'Lord, if it is you, tell me to come to you...' There is good evidence for God, but many may come to him still in some doubt about whether he even exists. The way to an inner assurance, however, is through action – speaking to God and asking to come to him.

What were the thoughts that rushed through Peter's mind before he stepped out? Was it really Jesus? What would his friends in the boat think? Suppose it didn't work, and he sank – how stupid he'd look! How could he face the storm, raging around them?

How many people since then have not come to Christ for fear of what their friends might think, or fear of the storms of persecution that might come, or fear that it might not work?

Peter started out, looking into the face of Jesus Christ. Perhaps he was tempted to look down at his feet to examine the great experience he was having. Had he done so, then he would have surely begun to sink, and so lost the experience altogether. Christians too may become so engrossed in examining themselves to see how their experience is developing, that it begins to leave them cold. If we keep looking towards the face of Jesus, the experience will take care of itself. Peter saw the strength of the gale and was seized with fear. Sinking, he cried: 'Save me, Lord', and was at once rescued. God's concern is that we should come, and if we begin to sink in fear, the Lord Jesus Christ will save us if we call to him.[150]

The whole secret is to keep looking towards Jesus Christ as we meet him day by day and find him in the Gospels. We need to leave the laughter of some friends behind us in the boat, walk through the storm, and let the experience take care of itself. Finally, a deep peace and joy in believing is left to us, as we

---

[150] Romans 10:13

know that Jesus has come to be with us and guide and stimulate us in the adventure of Christian living.

Summary

To become a Christian a person must begin talking personally to God, who is himself a person:

1. Confessing his or her failings and confirming a willingness to do God's will.

2. Thanking God for the forgiveness offered through Christ's work in dying for him or her.

3. Asking Christ to enter his or her life and share it.

He will.

It is good to put your prayer to God into your own words. Some people, however, may find this difficult at first, so here is a prayer of commitment which could be used:

Heavenly Father,

I am sorry that I have not come to you before, and I repent of not living in your world in your way. Now I want to do your will.

Please forgive me for the things that I have done wrong.

I thank you for sending your son Jesus, and accept his death for my wrongdoing. I accept your forgiveness and receive your son Jesus into my life as my Saviour and my Lord. I intend henceforward to live for you as his disciple.

Thank you for the help of your Holy Spirit in leading me to this point of decision. I ask you now for him to fill me with power to live and love for you day by day.

Amen.

Digging deeper

Digging deeper

Some recommended further reading.

1. About this book
2. Why bother about God?
3. What is the evidence for God?

● Roger T Forster & V Paul Marston, *Reason and Faith* (1989)
● Clive Calver, *Thinking Clearly about Truth* (1995)

4. Science: assertions and limits
5. Science, origins and chance

● Roger T Forster & V Paul Marston, *Reason and Faith* (1989)
● D J Bartholomew, *God of Chance* (1984)
● Jim Brooks, *Origins of Life* (1985)
● Rodney D Holder, *Nothing But Atoms and Molecules?* (1993)
● Arthur Peacocke, *Reduction in Academic Disciplines* (1985)
● John Polkinghorne, *Science and Creation* (1988)
● John Polkinghorne, *Science and Providence* (1989)
● John Polkinghorne, *Reason and Reality* (1991)
● John Polkinghorne, *Science and Christian Belief* (1994)
● John Polkinghorne, *Quarks, Chaos and Christianity* (1994)
● David Wilkinson, *God, the Big Bang and Stephen Hawking* (1993)
● John Wright, *Designer Universe* (1994)
● Michael Poole, *Science and Belief* (1990)

6. Has God been in touch?
7. A pattern in God's dealings?

● Roger T Forster & V Paul Marston, *God's Strategy in Human History* (1973 & 1989)
● Anis A Shorrosh, *Islam Revealed* (1988)
● F S Copleston, *Christ or Mohammed?* (1989)

8. Reliable sources?

● Roger T Forster & V Paul Marston, *Reason and Faith* (1989)
● Craig Blomberg, *The Historical Reliability of the Gospels* (1987)
● F F Bruce, *The Canon of Scripture* (1988)
● F F Bruce, *Jesus and Christian Origins Outside the New Testament* (1974)
● Allan Millard, *Discoveries From The Time Of Jesus* (1990)
● Carsten Thiede, *Jesus, Life or Legend* (1990)

9. Dead men tell no tales
10. Detective work and the resurrection

● Roger T Forster & V Paul Marston, *Reason and Faith* (1989)
● Val Grieve, *Your Verdict on the Empty Tomb of Jesus* (1988)
● Josh McDowell, *The Resurrection Proven Beyond Doubt!* (1988)
● John Wenham, *The Easter Enigma* (2nd edn., 1993)

11. I think therefore I am – I think...

● Roger T Forster & V Paul Marston, *Reason and Faith* (1989)
● John C Eccles and Karl Popper, *The Self and Its Brain* (1977)
● Mary Stewart Van Leeuwen, *The Person in Psychology* (1985)

12. It's a miracle!
● Roger T Forster & V Paul Marston, *Reason and Faith* (1989)
● Colin Brown, *Miracles and the Critical Mind* (1984)
● Peter Gammons, *Christ's Healing Power Today* (1992)
● Rex Gardner, *Healing Miracles, A Doctor Investigates* (1988)
● David Lewis, *Healing: Fiction, Fantasy or Fact?* (1989)
● Colin Urquhart, *Receive Your Healing* (5th imp., 1993)
● David Marshall, *Is God Still in the Healing Business?* (1994)

13. The experience of God
14. Over to you!
● John White, *When the Spirit Comes With Power* (rev. edn., 1992)
● Patrick Dixon, *Signs of Revival* (1994)
● Ted Harrison, *Stigmata: A Mediaeval Mystery for a Modern Age* (1994)
● Dave Roberts, *The 'Toronto' Blessing* (1994)
● Wallace Boulton (ed.), *The Impact of Toronto* (1995)
● Roger T Forster, *Finding the Path* (1989)
● Roger T Forster, *Saving Faith* (1984)

Index

Abraham, 51, 52, 54
Adam and Eve, 51
Afterlife, 88
Allegro, John, 46
Amino Acids, 37
Anderson, Norman, 63
Angels, appearance of, 79
Animism, 45
Archaeology, 61
Atkins, Peter, 28, 84
Authorised Version, 61
Ayala, F J, 83

Bacteria, 37
Barbour, Ian, 93
Barnabas, Gospel of, 63
Becoming a Christian, 108
Belief-systems, 21
Bethany, 77, 78, 79
Big Bang, 25
Big Foot, 15
Boyle, Robert, 24
Brooks, Jim, 40
Bruce, F F, 63, 66
Buddhism, 45

Campbell, Neil A, 41
Carbon, 34

Carey, George, 101
Cells, living
    eukaryotic, 37, 38, 41
    prokaryotic, 37, 41
Chance
    Chance$_1$=Probability, 30, 31, 32,
    33, 34, 37
    Chance$_2$=Undesigned, 31, 32,
    33, 36
    vs design (in past), 24
Charismatic Experience, 99
Chrestus, 65
Clark, Kelly J, 28
Claudius, 65
Cleopas, 77, 79
Coates, Gerald, 95
Codices of New Testament, 61
Consciousness, 81, 89
Croft, L R, 40
Crucifixion
    method of, 62
    Muslim view of, 48
    time of, 66

David, 50, 54
Davies, Paul, 35, 43
Dawkins, Richard, 28, 83, 84
Dead Sea Scrolls, 55, 64

Deedat, Ahmed, 48
Descartes, Rene, 82, 86
Determinism, 87
Disciples, the, 77, 79
DNA, 25, 37, 38
    E coli, 37
    human, 37
Dualistic Interactionism, 87

E coli bacterium, 37
Early Christian Writers, 62, 74
Eccles, John, 23, 86
Eddington, Arthur, 87
Einstein, Albert, 26, 85
Eukaryotic Cells, 37
Eusebius, 60
Evidence, lines of, 19
Eyewitness Accounts,
    nature of, 75

Faith, 109
Felix, Minucius, 24
Festus, 68, 70
Forster, Roger, 13
Fossils, 25
France, R T, 76
Future, 16

Gammons, Peter, 95
Gardner, Rex, 95
Gethsemane, 77
Gnostic 'Gospels', 63
God of the gaps, 42
Godel's Theorem, 84
Gospels
    authors of, 60
    date of, 63, 67, 74
Greek Orthodox, 102
Gribbin, John, 34

Hawking, Stephen, 27, 86
Herod, 77
Hewitt, J W, 62
Hinduism, 45
Holder, Rodney D, 84
Holy Spirit, 20
Hubble Space Telescope, 25
Hume, David, 83, 94

I think therefore I am, 81
Isaiah, 52, 54, 55, 57
Islam (see also 'Muslims'), 45, 46

James
    brother of Jesus, 71
    brother of John, 60
Jesus
    and non-Christian sources, 66
    and plot theories, 72
    and prophecy, 54
    arrest of, 77
    as Messiah, 53, 56
    as object of faith, 112
    Christian view of, 47
    identity of, 46, 56
    Muslim view of, 48
    non-Christian Jewish view of, 47
    relatives of, 77
    resurrection appearances of, 79
    resurrection of (see also
        'Resurrection'), 54, 68-74
    three views of, 46
    time of execution, 54, 66
    visions of, 99
    walking on the water, 111
Joanna, 77, 78
John, 47, 59, 60, 62, 66, 70, 76, 77,
    78, 79
Joseph of Arimathea, 71, 72

Josephus, 64
Judaism (or 'Jews'), 45, 46, 50, 56
Justin Martyr, 72, 74

Language, 23, 45, 93
Legends, nature of, 74, 80
Life
    age of, 25
    nature of, 37
    origins of, 36, 39, 40, 41
Logical Positivism, 27
Luke, 58, 59, 60, 61, 65, 70, 76, 78,
    79

MacKay, D M, 82, 86, 93
Marcus Aurelius, 83
Mark, 59, 60, 76, 79
Marshall, I Howard, 60
Marston, Paul, 13, 86
Mary
    Magdalene, 77, 78, 79
    mother of Jesus, 77
Matthew, 59, 60, 76, 78, 79
Messiah, 51, 52, 53, 56
Millard, Alan, 62, 64
Miller, S L, 40
Mind, 82, 83
Miracles
    Type-1, 90, 91
    Type-2, 90, 91, 92, 96
Mishnah, 46, 66
Monod, Jacques, 31
Morality, 16, 51
Moses, 51, 52
Multiple Universes, 36
Muslims (see also 'Islam'), 48, 50,
    57, 63

Nagel, T, 84

Natural Selection, 25
Nature (Journal), 41
Nero, 65
Nicodemus, 71, 72
Noah, 50, 51
Nothing Buttery, 82, 83
Nucleotides, 37

Papias, 76
Papyri of New Testament, 61
Passover, 51, 54, 66
Paul, Apostle, 20, 22, 24, 70
Peacocke, Arthur, 82
Penrose, Roger, 87
Personhood, 43
    of God, 15, 88, 107
    of us, 15, 88
Persons, 44
Perspectivalism, 86
Peter, 60, 77, 78, 79, 111
Physicalism, 21, 28, 84
Physics, 85
Planets, 37
Pliny, 65
Poole, Michael, 28
Popper, Karl, 23, 86
Powell, Enoch, 46
Prokaryotic Cells, 37
Proteins, 37
Psalms, 54
Purpose
    experience of, 23
    for universe, 15

Q (conjectured Gospel source), 59
Qur'ân, the Holy, 48, 50, 51, 55, 58

Reductionism, 82
Rees, Martin, 34

Religion, 14
Religious Experiences, 98
Resurrection of Jesus, 20
    Alternatives–Fraud, 72
    Alternatives–Hallucination, 73
    Alternatives–Hidden Meaning, 69
    Alternatives–Legend, 74
    Alternatives–Mistake, 71
    evidence for, 69
    Muslim view of, 48
    Purpose, 89
Right With God, 100
RNA, 37, 39
Robinson, John, 62, 76
Rylands Fragment, 61, 62

Sacrifice, 51, 54
Salome, 77
Schonfield, Hugh, 72
Science
    Faculties, 25, 26
    nature of, 92
Searle, John, 85
Smith, Morton, 47
Solar System, 25
Spong, John Selby, 70, 76
Suetonius, 65

Tacitus, 65
Talmud, 47, 66
Taoism, 45
Thiering, Barbara, 46, 70
Toronto Experience, 100
Tosh, John, 59
Translations (of New Testament), 62
Tree of Life, 89
Trigg, Roger, 85
Truth, nature of, 11

Uncertainty Principle, 87
Universe
    age of, 25, 26
Urquhart, Colin, 95

Vermes, Geza, 47
Viruses, nature of, 39
Von Daniken, Erich, 46

Wald, G, 41
Walker, B, 63
Ward, Keith, 28
Wenham, John, 59, 77, 100
Williamson, Hugh, 64
Wilson, E O, 84
Wilson. A N, 71
Wimber, John, 95
Wolfe, Stephen L, 40